Medieval Castles, Towers, Peles and Bastles
of Northumberland

by

T.H. ROWLAND, M.A. M.Ed. F. S.A(Scot)

To Gwen, companion to castles and typist.

SANDHILL
PRESS

Bamborough

First published in 1987 © T.H. Rowland
This reprint published in 1991 by Sandhill Press Ltd., 17 Castle Street,
Warkworth, Morpeth, Northumberland, NE65 0UW.

ISBN 0 946098 24 7

Printed by the Abbey Press, Hexham.

Contents

Welton Tower: Halton: Aydon Castle: Corbridge: Bywell.
Dilston: Blanchland: Hexhamshire and Hexham.
Conclusions.
Addenda.
Books and References, Index and Maps.
Note — Spellings vary enormously e.g. Exhamshire — Hexhamshire, and in the N.C.H. 1940 Tynedale is Tyndale.
Northumbrians spelled or spelt as they pronounced. Spelt also is corn and speld or spelk splinter, light, slice of wood.)

The Castle, from the County Court, Newcastle-on-Tyne

Castles — Introduction

Castles are a subject of perennial interest. They first came to England in 1066, introduced by William the Conquerer and his Norman army. Indeed they were an essential factor in the Conquest. A Castle was built within the walls of the Roman fort at Porchester and another at Hastings. The Bayeux Tapestry provides an illustration of the process — a "motte" is shown as constructed at Hastings, a great mound of earth on top of which was a circular stockade and timber tower. The word "motte" applies to both the embankment and ditch, but in English we tend to think of the ditch only as "moat".

In the same way the donjon was a keep or strong tower, the best example being the White Tower of London. The word comes from dominio meaning "power", and it was the Norman sign of power. The English tended to think of "dungeon", which was a basement or prison and to them a sign of conquest.

Castles in those times were a matter of life and death. The Normans depended upon these fortresses to maintain their hold on the country in face of a hostile population. In time castles were built by barons with royal permission. They might be held against each other or against the King. Early castles in Northumbria were held against the King, and in 1095 William II (Rufus) was occupied in taking castles at Bamburgh, Morpeth and Tynemouth.

For some five hundred years castles were of the greatest importance for the defence of the realm. Their development reached a climax in the reign of Edward I, whose Welsh Castles were masterpieces of military art and science. Guns and gunpowder made them more vulnerable, but they played their part in the Civil War of Charles I against Parliament in the seventeenth century. Cromwell's men "slighted" castles — levelled them and made them useless, hence Cromwell's reputation for making ruins.

In the following century castles acquired a romantic or poetic interest. Writers, artists and travellers were looking for the picturesque. Nothing could be more attractive than the ruins of a castle or monastery. Some landowners, who had no such relics, constructed them. These romantic ruins were called "follies", but were places of pleasure. In 1764 Horace Walpole wrote his "The Castle of Otranto", a story of dark deeds that occurred in castle vaults. Others wrote romantic tales and poems. Ballads were collected and even forged — living poets pretending that their work was medieval. Sir Walter Scott spent much of his time collecting ballads and ancient tales in the Minstrelsy of the Border. The Lay of the Last Minstrel and Marmion were romantic stories in verse, which had a huge circulation. But even more popular were his historical novels, in particular Ivanhoe, which recalled the deeds of gallant knights and evil men in the reigns of Richard I — the Crusader King — and his wicked brother, John. There were battles, tournaments and archery contests with Robin Hood and his Merrie Men. Scott also published volumes on the Antiquities of the Border, in which were illustrations of Castles, Churches and Monasteries.

Perhaps the climax of this interest was the Eglinton Tournament of 1839, early in the reign of Queen Victoria, who herself excited romantic interest. The Prime Minister, Lord Melbourne, had decided to drop a lot of expensive medieval pageantry from the coronation. This included the dramatic action of the Queen's Champion, fully armed and on horseback, throwing down the gauntlet during the banquet at Westminister Hall as a challenge to any person who opposed the Queen. Lord Eglinton, who might have had a part in this, consulted other young peers and it was decided to hold a full scale medieval tournament on his Scottish estates — similar to Scott's tournament at Ashby-de-la-Zouch as depicted in Ivanhoe. This would provide them with compensation and an opportunity for merry making.

Among those involved was the Marquis of Waterford, who had inherited Ford Castle from the Delaval Estates. His wife, daughter of Lord Stewart of Rothsay, was a very attractive lady and might have been the Queen of Beauty. The award, however, had to go to one unmarried — Lady Seymour. A crowd of 100,000 assembled for the occasion, but it was a wash-out from a terrible downpour that ruined the costumes and made tilting hazardous. The river flooded — tents and canopies leaked. Many had to spend the night in carriages, barns or haystacks. It was an expensive fiasco.

However, when Queen Victoria and Albert later planned their Highland retreat, it was Balmoral Castle, built in the old baronial style with towers and battlements.

John Dobson, the famous Newcastle architect of this time, designed prisons at Morpeth and Newcastle in authentic castle style, having made a special study of Edward I's Welsh Castles. His finest work was considered to be Beaufront Castle, for Aidan Cuthbert, overlooking Corbridge and the Tyne valley. This was built in castle style to replace the old Errington mansion.

Others added tall towers to their dwellings as at Eshot Hall and Little Harle tower. A tall square tower became a status symbol, often with a flag flying. Lady Waterford, after her husband's death, lived at Ford and restored to the Castle something of its medieval style, as did Salvin at Alnwick for the Duke of Northumberland in the mid nineteenth century.

Some castles are still residences and have been perhaps for 900 years. Others have disappeared or have been ruined. Some, an increasing number, have been preserved by English Heritage. Millions of people visit castles, and at various sites there can be jousting, archery, Norman mercenaries and mock sieges. War-gaming societies take the field and there are some thirty occasions of this kind every year at castle sites. Books on castles continue to appear from the press with associated books on heraldry, armour and weapons. Battlefields are also brought to the public notice with appropriate explanations — many of these are in Northumberland. In the Times newspaper, February 4th, 1987, we have the headline — "Baronet restores a ruined castle". Sir Humphry Wakefield proposes to live at Chillingham Castle in Northumberland, where in the Park are the wild white cattle. The castle was dilapidated and was last inhabited by troops in World War II. Now it is open to visitors in the summer months, increasing the number of castles that can be visited.

Hexham Market Place, Northumberland.

The Development of Castles

The original castles established by the Normans from 1066 were termed "motte and bailey" i.e. a dominating mound and a defended enclosure.

The motte had a timber stockade around the perimeter and in the centre was a tall timber tower like a citadel. From this the landscape could be scanned and the bailey covered by the fire of arrows — the axis was about 100 yards, so that the bailey could be extended, if necessary, all round the keep. Usually it was one segment, so that the castle was key or saddle shaped. Details of these castles have been discovered from pictures, such as the Bayeux Tapestry and by excavation as at Abinger.

Usually these timber castles have been replaced by stone, but from the first the Normans had stone castles at key points. The most important were the White Tower, London, the headquarters of the King, Rochester and Dover, which secured communications with Normandy across the Channel. All these were Roman sites as were many others like Porchester. Roman roads were the communications of the conquered kingdom.

The timber castles might be regarded as temporary, but they could last a long time. Dangers were fires lighted by attackers, but the timbers could be protected by earth. If the bailey were taken, the motte might still hold out till rescue came. Another danger was undermining to make the defences collapse, and castle builders had to develop defensive devices. The deep moat or ditch, whether dry or water-filled, always presented a considerable obstacle, and in the ditch attackers were in a most dangerous position. The ramparts or sides of the motte were made as steep as possible and we only see them after centuries of erosion. Extra protection could be provided by another palisade on the outside of the ditch. A further development was the shell keep — a strong stone wall was constructed round the perimeter of the motte on top of the mound and buildings were constructed within the walls. A very good example in Northumberland is Mitford Castle. Later developments often obscure the early origins of castles — observation of sites can be supplemented by historical information.

By 1100 A.D. Northumberland had a considerable number of castles. Bamburgh was the defended rock. Tynemouth was on a rocky headland with a ditch across the neck of the peninsula. Newcastle was constructed by Robert, son of William I, on the site of the Roman fort. In 1095, during the rebellion against William II, Bamburgh and Tynemouth were taken. From a French writer, Gaimar, we discover that the King

> "Le Nouvel-chastel, donc fermad
> Puis prist Morpathe un fort chastel
> Ki iert asis sur un muncel."

. . .   "Then strengthened the New castle,
> next took Morpeth, a strong castle
> Which was situated on a little mound."

The Umfravilles had castles at Prudhoe and Elsdon, one of the best examples of a motte and bailey in the country. At Bolam a prehistoric hill fort was used and may be the Camp House hill fort served for Walton. Warkworth and Alnwick obtained early castles and the mottes are still visible. Others were at Norham and Wark upon Tweed. There were mottes, still visible now at Warden and Gunnerton. Mitford has already been mentioned, and there were probably others which were the heads of baronies. Wark-on-Tyne Castle is an impressive mound capped by a farmhouse, and Bellingham disappeared. There is a mound that might be a motte at Lowick Steads and another in the fields near Fenham Mill. It was captured by Colonel Fenwick for Parliament in the Civil War, when many castles suffered.

Norman Kings were not too keen on barons building strong castles and royal approval was needed. But in Stephen's reign (1135-1154) when there was civil war between his supporters and those of Matilda, Henry I's daughter, the barons built castles as they pleased, and the King of Scots took over Tynedale as his own. The Anglo Saxon Chronicle records for 1137 — "When the traitors perceived that he (Stephen) was a mild man, gentle and did them no justice, they all wondered. They had done homage and sworn him oaths, but they held no troth. They were all forsworn and their oaths abandoned, for every powerful man made his castles and then held them against him and filled the land full of castles. They oppressed the wretched men of the land hard with work on the castles and when the castles were made they filled them with devils and evil men. They they took the people they believed had any goods, both by night and by day, men and women and put them in prison: they were after gold and silver and tortured them with unspeakable tortures, for never were the martyrs tortured as they were. Men hung them by the feet and smoked them with foul smoke." It was said that God and His Saints slept.

There were manor houses or halls that were not fortified, though surrounded by ditch and ramparts which could be made defensible. Originally many of these were of timber, and there are sites of this kind in Northumberland consisting of medieval enclosures where the buildings have disappeared.

Henry II (1154-1189), Matilda's son, who succeeded Stephen, re-asserted the authority of the King and unlicensed castles were destroyed. Where they were necessary, the barons might keep their strongholds on payments of fines. This was the time for the building of massive keeps as at Newcastle upon Tyne, and the town was defended with stone walls. The keep still stands 75 feet high, other dimensions being 62 feet by 56 feet. It was a royal castle and Maurice the engineer, who worked at Dover, was mainly responsible. It was built between 1172 and 1177, costing £911-10-9.

Bamburgh also gained a keep 69 feet by 61 feet, but only 55 feet high. Since it stood high on solid rock a basement was not necessary unlike Newcastle where entrance was the the second floor.

At Norham, overlooking the Tweed, Bishop Hugh de Puiset of Durham built a great keep standing 90 feet high, its other dimensions being 84 by 60 feet.

Prudhoe had a keep by 1173 being 44 feet by 41 feet and about 50 feet high. It withstood a determined attack by the Scots under William the Lion, who was later captured at Alnwick.

Since England was connected with the continent and Henry II ruled a large part of France, architectural ideas were transferred. His son Richard the Lion Heart was engaged in a Crusade and acquired more ideas on castle building. His great castle of Chateau Galliard in France was, in its day, a model of scientific fortification. It had an outer ward, inner ward and the keep complex with its own walled enclosure. The castle had interval mural towers projecting from the curtain walls and round towers at the sensitive corners or angles. In spite of its strength it was taken by the French after a long siege in the reign of King John.

To understand the development of castles, it is necessary to look at methods of attack and defence. Many of these derived from the Romans. The ballista was an example of this — it was like a giant crossbow on wheels and could fire huge bolts with tremendous force. There was a catapult type of machine, again on wheels. It consisted of a large spoon-like piece of apparatus, the narrow end being embodied in coiled ropes, which tightened as the wide end was pulled down to ground level where it was loaded with stones or debris. When the catches were released the arm with load flew up with tremendous force and hurled its ammunition against the walls of the castle, or over them. Another was the slinging machine which consisted of a strong timber frame on which a long wooden limb was pivoted near its base. To this was attached a large, heavy container of earth as a balance weight. When at rest this hung low and the long arm stood vertical with sling-sack attached to its top end. To load the apparatus the arm was pulled down by a winch and the counter-weight raised. The sling was loaded and when the counterweight was released, the stones were flung with great force. These machines were not very accurate, but could be a great nuisance to defenders.

The most successful method for attackers could be undermining defences. First the moat had to be filled, before battering rams or other equipment could be brought against the walls. Continual fire was kept up by archers from behind protecting mantlets, and the battering ram itself was housed in a wheeled penthouse for protection. The ram had an iron head and it was swung backwards and forwards against the wall. The defenders might lower sacks of earth or wool or matting to lessen the impact.

The corners of walls or towers were most vulnerable because corner stones could be prised out and others followed. While it was being undermined masonry could be held up by wooden props. When sufficient penetration was made these could be fired, bringing about the collapse of the wall. Round towers were not vulnerable in this way and were more difficult to hit with missiles, which tended to glance away. There were no weakening corners. The mural towers of the castle provided a method of angle fire, so that attackers could be hit at the base of the wall. If the wall were entirely straight, defenders would have to look out and be exposed. The tops of walls were embattled or crenellated. This consisted of pieces of upstanding masonry called merlons and gaps called embrasures, which could be covered with flaps.

The base of a tower or gate could be vulnerable, because beneath them the enemy were difficult to hit. There developed what was called machicolation — a series of brackets projecting from walls and carrying a gallery. These could be stone or timber, and holes can still be seen in castle walls for such timbers. The gallery projected over the wall and missiles could be fired. All kinds of things, solid and liquid could be poured through the floor of the gallery onto attackers. The outer wall had a projection at the right height to send what was dropped outwards against the persons of the attackers.

A "license to crenellate" from the King was necessary, so that a castle could be made fully defensible. Usually a comparatively small number of defenders could withstand an attack from a much larger force. To withstand a seige defenders had to be plentifully supplied with food, weapons and water. There were wells within the castle walls, both in the courtyard and the castle itself.

Archers defending the castle were provided with loopholes in the mural and gate towers. Outwardly they appear as long slits in the masonry, running vertically with fish tails and cross loops, to allow firing at different angles and levels. Behind the loop is a recess in the masonry to allow the presence of archers. These were crossbowmen, who could fire very accurately, and each would be provided with a loader. Long bows were not used until after the Welsh wars and then preferably on the field of battle.

The entrance to the castle was defended by a strong tower, approached by a drawbridge which could be raised. Extra strength was provided by an iron portcullis that was let down, so that if the timberwork of the doors was burnt, there was still no entry. Guard rooms were situated on either side of the tunnel entrance, which had "murder holes" in the ceiling. There was a second set of defences at the end of a tunnel. Attackers, surprisingly, might find entrance before the bridge was lifted or the portcullis fell — only to find themselves in a trap and eliminated to a man.

Edward I (1275-1307), was one of the greatest warriors of all time. He fought as a Prince in England against rebels, in France against the enemy and he also took part in a Crusade to the Holy Land. So he was an expert on war and fortification, besides being a man of law.

He decided to bring peace to the Borders, and invaded Wales with the skill of the Roman Agricola. Wales was reduced and castles were built at strategic places to complete the conquest. The castles were the climax of fortification before the coming of gunpowder and cannon. Edward also established towns with castles and walled defences. To bring about the conquest of Wales, he required men from every county, not only soldiers but castle builders.

Northumberland provided him with 50 men, and these and soldiers returning home from the Welsh Wars would bring back with them the latest ideas of fortification. This can be seen in the castles of the fourteenth century, which were all the more necessary because Edward I provoked the Scottish Wars. Given a longer life "the Hammer of the Scots" might have been successful, but his incompetent son floundered to defeat at Bannockburn, and was unable to organize the defences of the country. The borderers had to fend for themselves and built their own castles and fortresses. Towers were erected all over the county for local self defence.

In 1309 the Percies, whose main base had been in Yorkshire, acquired Alnwick from Bishop Bek, strengthening the fortifications of the Castle. They also acquired Warkworth and had castles at Prudhoe and Langley. During the fourteenth century they greatly increased their wealth and power, extending their territory into Scotland. They were, however, engaged in rebellion, and Harry Hotspur was killed in 1403. His father, the Earl of Northumberland, was defeated in 1405, when the fortifications of Warkworth were shattered. Strongly defended by river and terrain from the north against the Scots, it was easy to bring up cannon from the south by the English King against a rebel.

Thomas Earl of Lancaster led the opposition to Edward II. He had great castles at Pontefract and Dunstanburgh, which was to be his retreat. He was killed at Boroughbridge in 1322.

Other castles were built such as Belsay and Chipchase. These were tower-houses. Ford and Chillingham had a different plan, being quadrangular with square towers at each corner. Buildings adjoined the curtain wall and there was an open courtyard in the centre. Ravines, rivers and man-made ditches added to the defences. At other places such as Aydon, Shortflatt and Haughton castles were strongly fortified. More and more towers were built with fortified enclosures called "peles" from the French. By misnomer the name was carried to the towers themselves. The English built castles in Scotland as at Hermitage and Roxburgh. Roxburgh was a very powerful fortress and King James II of Scotland was killed in 1460 by an exploding cannon, which he brought against it.

In 1415, at the beginning of the reign of Henry V, a list was compiled of what were called the Castles and Fortalices of the land. A distinction is made between the castrum (strong fort or castle) and fortalicium (lesser fort). 37 Castles are listed and 78 Fortalices — 115 in all and this is not the total number. While Henry V was at war in France, the Scots might take advantage of the situation. So it was to the advantage of every local lord and landowner to see to his defences. The older hall house was a long rectangular building with several compartments, including accommodation for cattle and horses. It has been said that the tower house that developed was the hall house up-ended, with a series of floors one above the other. The remarkable feature of the building was its height. On the ground floor was the store and possibly the kitchen. It was ventilated by narrow loops. The walls were very thick and the floor was stone vaulted. The door could be reinforced by an iron "yett". The first floor contained the hall and solar, or private apartment. Above on the next floor were the bedchambers and higher still the rampart walk and the roof. Some had extra rooms at this level by adding walls within the rampart and a pointed roof — this can be seen at Shortflatt Tower or Elsdon Vicar's Pele.

Some of the larger tower houses in Northumberland had corbelled bartizans at each corner. Extra defences could be provided by the addition of double moats on lower lying land. Examples are at Ogle on the river Blyth and Horton Castle near the sea above Blyth. This belonged to Guiscard de Charron, a justice in Northumberland in Edward I's reign.

After years of success in France, the English were eventually defeated and driven out, except for Calais (1454). This was taken by the French at the end of Mary's reign 1558. For a period of thirty years, from 1454 to 1485, England was torn by Civil War between the rival royal houses of Lancaster and York, commonly called the Wars of the Roses. This unhappy period ended with the victory of Henry Tudor over Richard III at the Battle of Bosworth (1485).

Some castles such as Bamburgh, Dunstanburgh and Warkworth suffered severely, since cannons were used against them. They might be battered and captured, repaired and then lost to opposing forces. Some castles and towers declined in importance, but others had to be maintained for the defence of the Scottish Border.

In 1496 James IV invaded England to support the Pretender, Perkin Warbeck, and again in 1513 before the Battle of Flodden.

A number of castles were attacked and badly damaged, such as Twizell, Ford and Etal. Later in his reign Henry VIII after his quarrel with the Pope and the Dissolution of the Monasteries feared invasion. He constructed a number of coastal forts including Beblowe Castle on Holy Island. But he was also concerned with the defence of the Border, and in 1541 a special survey was made — View of the Castles, Towers, Barmkins and Fortresses of the Frontier of the East and Middle Marches by Sir Robert Bowes and Sir Ralph Ellerker.

It is noticeable that the word 'pele' is only twice used for either tower or enclosure. The report was on the condition of the "castells, towres and fortresses" and how they might be repaired. It covered the area north and west of a line from Langley, Haughton, Rothley, Crawley, Chillingham to Haggerston, roughly within twenty miles of the Border. The government was also anxious to encourage enclosures with hedges and ditches to impede the Scots, who could range much more freely over country that was open.

The report showed that large areas of land were deserted as "waste" and many buildings had been destroyed by wars or raiding. Altogether 115 castles, towers and fortresses were listed. Of these 48 were given as ruinous, lacking repair or cast down by the King of the Scots. These included some of the most important castles and towers — Tilmouth, Heaton, Wark, Howtell, Twizell, Etal, Ford, Hepple, Harbottle, Haughton, Sewingshields, Blenkinsop, Langley and Tarset. The authors were most anxious about the existence or construction of barmkins for the safety of people, possessions and cattle. Some examples can be quoted — Heaton is a ruinous castle "defaced by the warres", but it could be repaired. At East Newton was a "lytle towre and a stone house" joined to it, but this was too low and had been burnt by the Scots. It was recommended that the walls should be much higher. Middleyon Hall had in it "two stone houses or bastells". Akeld had "a lytle fortelett or bastle house without a barmekyn". Fowberry tower was in good repair, but had no barmkin.

There seems to have been a shortage of suitable timber in the north and supplies could be shipped to Holy Island or Tweedmouth. A tower would cost £100 to construct and a barmkin £200. Norham Castle was in good repair, but at Twizell the walls of the fortress were as cast down by the King of the Scots and so was Duddo. Both Etal and Ford, burnt by the King of Scots in 1513, were still in need of repair. The vicar's pele at Ford had been raised "two houses highte" and should be higher to be safe — 3 houses (or floors) high. The owners, it was said, retired to safer places and avoided the expense of exposed places. Lowick, Alnham and Whittingham each had two towers, one in each village belonging to the vicar. There were vicar's towers at Ancroft, Embleton, Ingram and Alwinton. The castle of Harbottle was in great decay and this was royal property, but "Cartington is a good fortress of two towers and other strong stone houses", kept in good repair. The parsonage of Rothbury at Whitton was a tower and a little barmkin, both in good repair, but Tosson tower was decayed.

At Ritton and Greenleighton, formerly Newminster property and belonging to the King, the little stone houses and barmkins were not in repair. But Rothley tower was and "At Harterton Hall is a strong bastell house" of Sir John Fenwick in good repair. At Fawns "is a little pele house or bastell" of the same owner in good repair, and so was Wallington "a strong tower and stone house". At Gunnerton, too, he had a tower and stone house in good condition. Chipchase had a fair tower and a manor of stone work. At Simonburn is a "strong toure of foure house height" belonging, as did Chipchase, to the Herons. This seems to have been of the approved height. But at Haughton "standeth the walles of an olde castell of fortresse very strong but the roofes and floores thereof bene decayed and gone." It was the property of Sir John Widdrington and the barmkin was also ruinous. Willimoteswick had a good tower and stone house. Thirlwall, Blenkinsop and Featherstone are described as towers, but Bellister as a bastle. Langley Castle, belonging to the Earl of Northumberland, had nothing remaining but the walls.

In Tynedale there were no towers but one at Hesleyside. Tarset Hall had been burnt, and the old castle at Wark was gone. The men of Tynedale lived in inaccessible areas, cut by "ravins" and protected by fallen trees. "In which natural strength and fortifications of such places almost inaccessible the said Tyndales do much rejoice and embolden themselves and when they be affrayed do rather trust in the strengthe of such places without their houses than to the surety or defence of their houses. And yet surely the headsmen of them have very strong houses whereof for the most part the utter sides or walls be made greatt sware oak trees strongly bound and joined together with great tenons and the same so thick morticed that it will be very harde without great force and laboure to break or cast down any of the said houses the timber as well of the said walls as roofs be so greatt and covered most parte with turves and erth that they will not easily burn or be set on fire."

It seems that after the survey very little was done to repair fortifications, but in the last years of Henry VIII from 1542 and the first years of Edward VI, his son, there were campaigns in Scotland, and the Scots were defeated in battle. A report of Sir Robert Bowes, made in 1550, said — ". . for the most parte the fortresses, towres and piles upon the utter side or frontier of those east marches have been in tymes past rased and casten downe by the Scottes and yet be not repaired which is muche pitty to see", as the Castle of Heton, the towers of Twizell, Shoreswood, Barmoor, Duddo and others. They should be "amended, otherwise it will be great danger if the Scottes shall be hereafter able and of poure to invade those marches and remain any tyme in the same without repulse." Meanwhile strong houses of stone were still being built, encouraged by the government.

In 1970 the Royal Commission on Historical Monuments published a book called "Shielings and Bastles". Shielings were summer pastures with temporary dwellings. Bastles were the strong stone houses built during the period after 1541. The definition of the authors does not necessarily fit previous usage of the word. They say "Bastles show some variations, but on the whole they are remarkably uniform and several elements in common which distinguish them from peles and towers on the one hand and from more conventional buildings on the other. The typical bastle is rectangular on plan with external dimensions of about 35 feet by 25 feet: it is of two full storeys and has quite steeply pitched gables. The walls are built of stone in large blocks of irregular shape, the gaps between the blocks being packed with small stone chippings set in weak mortar with very little lime; they are about 4 feet thick on the ground floor, thinning to about 3½ feet at first floor level".

Entry was through a narrow door in the gable end at ground level. Access to the upper floor might be a ladder inside or outside. Sometimes there was a spiral stair within. The upper floor often consisted of large paving type stones laid across rough hewn timbers. These buildings could be regarded as farm houses and sometimes they were grouped together. Sixty were listed in the survey within 20 miles of the Border and others have since been discovered in wide areas of the county.

It is considered that there might be several hundred with many amalgamated into later farm buildings. While these individual defences were being built by lesser men, the government of Elizabeth I was engaged in the biggest defensive exercise of the age — the construction of the walls and bastions of Berwick. The scheme was based on the continental models of the time and provide a fitting climax to fortification and defence of the Border. Strangely enough, changes in religious and political views of the two countries, made them unnecessary while the little bastles still served against the reivers of the Border. Strong stone houses were still being built in the reign of James I.

Selections of Northumberland's Castles, Towers, Peles and Bastles

The total number, to my knowledge, is something like 500, and this is by no means complete.

There are many buildings in remote areas reduced to heaps of stones and it is impossible to say whether they might be a shepherds' cottages, farmsteads or field barns. Barns have been converted into houses and houses have been converted into barns. At Bradford, near Belsay, there is the example of an Elizabethean Hall of the Ogles, (G.O. 1567 on the fireplace), which has been converted long ago into a barn. A field barn on a hill near Black Heddon could have been a bastle. Many of these have been lost in farm buildings. The base of the bastle was the refuge for animals and in some places it still is. There are groups of strong houses in places like Wall, Eviestones and West Thornton. They are scattered over the Otterburn Military Range and the old Rothbury Forest. So there has to be a selection depending on accessibility and the visual quality of the building. It is always interesting to compare an empty building with one that is still used or inhabited.

Another problem is the matter of sequence in any account. An alphabetical list becomes a catalogue and one has to jump from place to place. I have preferred to connect buildings in an area or to each other in such a way that their construction makes sense, especially in considering matters of communication when there were border raids. Watch and ward had to be kept and beacons gave warning at night of approaching danger. Walls, hedges and ditches were hindrances to attackers, but the area around a castle or tower would be free from trees that provided cover. Macduff's men moving down to attack Macbeth at Dunsinane brought Birnam Wood with them as cover to confuse.

In looking at the fortifications of Northumberland, it is perhaps best to start with the Border, which was established with great difficulty in what was called "Debateable Land". Hadrian, the Roman Emperor, decided on a frontier from Newcastle to Carlisle, but the medieval frontier was angled with the Cumbrian section a little north of Carlisle and the Northumberland section reaching the Tweed at Berwick, some 65 miles north of Newcastle.

BERWICK, north of the Tweed, had changed hands thirteen times before it finally became English in 1483. It was a Scottish burgh and port with a great deal of trade. Henry II destroyed the castle of timber there and built one of stone, as at Newcastle. Richard I, however, sold it back to the Scots in order to raise money for his Crusade. King John started to build a castle at Tweedmouth, but the Scottish King paid him to have it discontinued since it would threaten his port.

In 1216, after the Scots supported the rebellious barons, John attacked Berwick and did much damage. (He also destroyed Morpeth and Mitford). There followed a long period of peace till Edward I asserted his claim to Scotland and hoped to gain control by a puppet king, John Balliol. In 1296, after damage to English shipping, Edward attacked and sacked Berwick. He built a castle and town walls, but these were not completed and Wallace took the town, but not the castle. Edward recovered the town and strengthened the walls. Berwick was captured by Robert Bruce in 1317 — the town developed high walls with 19 towers and the castle stood high to the west. In 1333, after his victory at Homildon Hill, Edward III regained the town, but it was lost for a time in 1355, while he was occupied in France. It was recovered, but lost again by Richard II and then recaptured. In 1461 during the Wars of the Roses it was surrendered by Henry VI, but regained by Richard, Duke of York, in 1483 and remained English.

Henry VII brought about a marriage alliance between his daughter Margaret and James IV of Scotland. He also had a bridge built over the Tweed, and looked forward to a union of the two countries. But there was much more trouble before this came about. Warfare continued under Henry VIII, and he added towers to Berwick's walls and built the Lord's Mount. Towers were added on the North west of the Castle. Edward VI constructed the New Fort or Citadel. The walls were difficult to keep in repair, and in Elizabeth's reign, in face of continued danger from Scotland, it was decided to shorten the perimeter. Hence the famous Elizabethan walls, built in the most up to date military fashion at great expense, when they were not really necessary.

Sir Richard Lee, who had served at Calais and knew about continental methods of defence, was sent to Berwick to provide fortifications, but the original plan was abandoned in favour of more advanced ideas and exploitation of the earthen rampart. Berwick was a great urban fortification and very different from any private affair. The work was costly and there were disputes with the Italian experts about the positions of batteries, the slope of the walls and the banks. It was the work of professionals and the final word in fortifications of that time, although never completed.

The northern third of the town and the castle were not included in the defences, which consisted of a number of bastions, shaped like arrow heads. They were designed in such a way as to cover each other with cross fire. The north and east sides were protected by these, linked by new walls. The medieval walls still covered the riverside. The old walls and the castle to some extent were used to provide stone. The new land-ward defences were nearly three quarters of a mile in length, took ten years of labour and cost some £129,000. There was a wide ditch and a thick rampart faced with stone. The five bastions were at key points — Meg's Mount, Cumberland Bastion, Brass Bastion, Windmill Bastion and King's Bastion. The walls of Berwick can be walked and provide excellent views of the river, port and town. The eighteenth century barracks have been preserved as a military museum.

The Castle has not been so fortunate, rather neglected from Elizabethan times and finally ruined by the railway. In its time it was strong and impressive. A Frenchman, Jorvin, paid a visit to Berwick and his description (1672) of the Castle is as follows.

On the hilltop "there is a ruined and abandoned castle, although its situation makes it appear impregnable; it is environed on one side by the ditch of the town; on the other side, by one of the same breadth, flanked by many round towers and thick walls, which inclose a large palace; in the midst of which rises a lofty keep, or donjon, capable of a long resistance and commanding all the environs of the town."

He explored the town and

"by walking over Berwick, I discovered it to be one of the greatest and most beautiful towns in England."

He admired the merchants' houses, the ships by the quay, and especially the bridge.

"There is not a stone bridge in all England longer or better built than that of Berwick, which has (15) sixteen large and wonderfully wrought arches; it is considered as one of the most remarkable curiosities in the kingdom."

It was constructed in the reign of James VI and I, who after being prostrated by fear of the old shaking timber bridge, required a new one to be built. In a way it illustrated the union of the two kingdoms. The King James Bridge lost its uniqueness in 1850 when Robert Stephenson's Royal Border Bridge was completed to carry the railway high above the river. It looks like a Roman aqueduct and is one of the glories of crossing the Border. It is 720 yards long and rises 126 feet above the water. There are 28 arches including a curve on the south side on the landward approach to the river.

Unfortunately the Castle suffered and it was mostly removed to make way for the station, providing much of the stone. Newcastle Keep was not plundered in the same way and gives some idea of what Berwick Castle might have been like, towering over the Tweed. It would not have had the railway passing at midfloor level as at Newcastle.

Berwick Castle had many royal visitors; but Queen Victoria passed its ruins over the Border Bridge, through the ghost of the Great Hall, where in 1292 Edward I made his award to John Balliol. All that now remains is the White Wall, which falls steeply by stages down the cliff side, flanked by the "Breakneck Stairs". It ends with a sixteenth century gun tower by the river. The ruins can be viewed from a park to the west, down which the path is more gentle, and it is pleasant to walk along the riverside and admire the bridges at different levels. Water levels rise with flood and tide, so that crossing the Tweed was difficult until a firm bridge was built. Berwick is famous for its swans and its salmon fishing. Looking up to the ruins of the castle we are reminded of the words of John Jarvie (1907) —

"Massive tower and graceful turret are gone, and in their place remain but a few ruins and a dismal looking station that cannot claim to be even modern. Yet even in its downfall and decay this ruined stronghold, for which rivers of blood have flowed and brave men have yielded up their lives by the thousands, is rich in interest and suggestiveness and could its crumbling walls but speak, many a tale would they unfold of battle, siege and escape by swift flowing river."

Norham on Tweed

Norham is situated on the Tweed some seven miles to the west of Berwick, and in time past belonged to the patrimony of Saint Cuthbert. So in Norman times and for centuries afterwards it belonged to the Bishop of Durham.

The Castle, despite the assaults of war and time, is still a very impressive sight. It caught the eye of Turner, the painter, and also the imagination of Sir Walter Scott, poet and historian in his "Marmion". Marmion was a Lincolnshire knight who was given a golden crested helmet by his lady and told to seek fame and fortune in the most dangerous place in England. This was considered to be Norham Castle, frequently attacked by the Scots, but not taken. There he was bound to be involved in fighting. At the time of his arrival, the governor was Sir Thomas Grey, who gave him his chance a few days later when a Scottish force arrived at the gates of the Castle. Wearing his golden crest Marmion charged on horseback into the enemy. He fought gallantly, but was wounded and unhorsed. The governor and his men came out to rescue him. He was rehorsed and helped in the defeat and rout of the Scots. There were many such adventures in these parts.

The Castle, built of reddish sandstone, stands high guarding a crossing of the Tweed. Today trees disguise the precipitous slopes to the north and east of the Castle, down to the river and into a ravine respectively. It overlooks the village of Norham to the west and has a deep ditch to the west and the south. The Marmion gate is situated at the N.W. angle and was the strongly guarded entrance to the Castle. There was also a very large outer enclosure.

The original castle was of the motte and bailey type. The motte carried timber work defences and was built by Bishop Flambard of Durham. It was destroyed by the Scots in the reign of Stephen and rebuilt on the orders of Henry II by Bishop Hugh de Puiset with strong walls and a great stone keep like Newcastle. The mason for Norham was Richard of Wolviston, who probably worked at Durham Castle. At times Norham was held by the King himself. It was always in the front line of attack by the Scots, but did not change hands like Berwick. It was subject to frequent additions and repairs, which can be seen by inspecting the site.

The keep is situated at the north east corner of the Castle, protected by the steep banks of the Tweed and a ravine. Within the enclosure it is protected by walls and a deep ditch. This had its own drawbridge and barbican. Within the inner bailey are the ruins of the great hall with the great chamber at one end and kitchens at the other. The keep measures 84 feet by 60 feet and was originally two storeys above a barrel vaulted basement, strongly built. It was raised two further storeys in the fifteenth century, so that walls still stand to a height of 90 feet. A cross wall was inserted in the basement to carry the extra weight. It was badly battered in 1513 by the guns of James IV before the fatal battle of Flodden. Mons Meg was used and could fire a ball of stone or iron weighing three hundredweights. Some of the cannon balls that were fired can be found in the basement. This battering accounts for the ruined wall on the north, though it was rebuilt after the battle and continued in use till the union of the two crowns made its upkeep unnecessary.

It had many associations with the Crown, since Kings from both sides of the Border were here. Here Edward I had been accepted by the Scottish Lords as arbitrator in the disputed succession to the Scottish Crown. John Balliol swore fealty to him after the award was made.

The Castle will repay a detailed inspection, having served in war for nearly five hundred years. Marmion's gate or the West Gate is not now the official entrance, but the best view of the keep is through its archway. A wooden bridge now replaces the drawbridge, and in the walls can be seen emplacements for cannon, the latest form of defence. Towers were added to the inner bailey overlooking the deep moat. Clapham's Tower, built in 1513, had gun ports. Water could be let into the inner moat. The outer bailey had a strong wall with a number of towers from Marmion's gate on the west to Sandurs Tower on the east. There was a southern entrance at the Sheep Gate with a drawbridge, now replaced by a causeway. The Custodian's house is adjacent to this gate, and the Castle is now in the care of English Heritage.

Norham is an attractive village with a church that dates back to Norman times. Over the Tweed at Ladykirk is an interesting Renaissance Church built by James IV, where he attended service before crossing the river for a campaign which led to the field of Flodden in 1513. Before this battle he had taken Wark, Ford and Etal Castles.

"Day set on Norham's castled steep,
And Tweed's fair river, broad and deep
And Cheviot's mountains lone:
The battled towers, the donjon keep
The loophole grates, where captives weep,
The flanking walls that round it sweep
In yellow lustre shone.
The warriors on the turrets high,
Moving athwart the evening sky,
Seem'd forms of giant height:
Their armour, as it caught the rays,
Flashed back again the western blaze,
In lines of dazzling light.

"Saint George's banner, broad and gay,
Now faded, as the fading ray
Less bright, and less was flung;
The evening gale had scarce the power
To wave it on the Donjon Tower,
So heavily it hung.
The scouts had parted on their search,
The castle gates were barr'd:
Above the gloomy portal arch,
Timing his footsteps to a march,
The warder kept his guard;
Low humming, as he paced along,
Some ancient Border gathering song."

Marmion: Canto I.

Twizell

Three miles westwards from Norham was the old Twizell Castle in a dominant position and overlooking the River Till. Beneath it and arched like a rainbow, was Twizell Bridge. It still stands today, now bypassed, after a 'reign' of 500 years. English troops used it before Flodden, and it is a fine example of medieval building. Spanning 90 feet, it seems to rise the same height to its apex above the river. It makes a romantic picture, with the ruins of a later Twizell Castle amid the trees above the cliff face.

Pevsner describes it as "a thickly ivy-laden and tree covered ruin of a monster folly, the house which Sir Francis Blake began about 1770 and never finished."

In 1812 it was five storeys high and was meant to rise a further fifteen feet. Wyatt was then working at Twizell Castle. Sir Francis gave a turret of the old castle to Count St Paul for re-erection at his mansion of Ewart Park and this still stands. Twizell Castle is a rectangular building like the medieval hall house. It had round towers at the corners, although two of these have gone since that time.

The masonry is of excellent quality and reddish sandstone was used. The basements are vaulted, but not below ground, and are still in good condition. These lower apartments are still perfectly dry, but the upper floors have disappeared. North of the Castle what appears to be the barmkin area was converted into gardens. There are excellent views towards the Border and southwards over the River Till. Sir Francis has been repeatedly condemned for his foolish waste of money, which made him bankrupt. However, he provided work for many over a long period at a time when there was much unemployment. The ruined Castle now could be mistaken for a medieval monument and is well worth a visit. The property belongs to the Tillmouth Hotel and Tillmouth Park, now demolished, was another Blake construction.

In 1541 it was reported

"At Twysle near unto the said ryver or castell rased and caste downe by the Kinge of Scots in a warre 40 yeres & more since".
In 1561 at Twizell "There hath beene in the said towne one towre or pile which is of ancjent tyme decayed and caste downe, and there remaineth one part or quarter thereof, and a barmkin about it."
These descriptions could apply to the present ruins, in the base of which the above ruins are embodied.

Cornhill

In 1541 "The tower of Cornell (Cornhill) standing upon the banke of the sayde river of Twede inyt be 12 husbandlandes well plenished and a tower new embattled, covered & put in good reparacon by one Gilbert Swynnoe gentleman, the owner . . . . of the said tower & towne of Cornell, who entendeth also as his powers may serve to buylde a barmkyn about the said tower & doth prepare stuffe for the same & the said barmkyn . . ."
It was considered that it would be a great help for the defence of the neighbourhood. Later Scots damaged it, so that now it has practically disappeared.

Wark upon Tweed

Wark is about eight miles to the west of Norham, situated at a convenient crossing of the Tweed by fording the river. A battle was fought near this place in 1018, and many since that date. The Castle was probably established about 1100 A.D. on a mound overlooking the river and village. A Chronicler wrote of "Carham which by the English is called Wark". This is the pronunciation of the word "work", a building or construction i.e. the castle. So the settlement was renamed.

Originally the barony belonged to Walter Espec, lord of Helmsley, Yorkshire. In Stephen's reign the Castle was several times besieged by King David of Scotland, and it was only taken after a long siege, when the defenders were starved after eating the last horse. Between 1158 and 1161 Henry II rebuilt the castle which had been razed to the ground. In 1174 William the Lion went to take the Castle of Wark, but failed and passed on. Returning later, he failed again. In 1215 it was burnt by the English King John, since the owner Robert Roos had signed Magna Carta. It was rebuilt and later held under royal control.

Edward I was there on a number of occasions. In the reign of Edward II it suffered severely and afterwards, when leased, was frequently attacked. In 1399 Sir Thomas Grey had his house burnt and his Castle walls beaten down. In 1460, during the Wars of the Roses, the Scots again demolished the Castle. In Tudor times, however, it was to reach the climax of its importance.
The Earl of Northumberland called it "the stay and key of all this country" . . . . "situate for annoyance and defence in the best place of all the frontiers".

It was held by the Grey family, but in 1513 it was taken by James IV. In 1517 Lord Dacre claimed £480 for its restoration. The keep or donjon was built 4 storeys high, in each of which except the top, were "five great murder holes . . . . so that great bombards can be shot from each of them". Trapdoors in each floor and a hoist would provide the necessary supplies. There was accommodation for 40 foot soldiers. The defences of both the inner and outer wards were to be strengthened. The inner curtain wall was to have an iron gate in a vaulted entrance, high enough to admit men on horseback. Built on to this was to be a two storey building big enough to house 140 men on the upper floor, six to a chamber. Beneath were stables for the horses — 12 to a stable. There was to be a hall with kitchen, bakehouse and other offices.

A well provided water for the garrison and accommodation could be found for a flock of sheep and 8 score beasts at night or in time of raids. The gatehouse was built 3 storeys high, and the gate was large enough to admit loads of hay. It contained the porter's lodge, and another tower was built at the point where the curtain wall touched the river Tweed. Lord Dacre wanted another tower on the west to protect the postern, to allow sallies out and provisions in. The outer ward could be a place of refuge for inhabitants and could accommodate 1,000 horses and cattle. Four gunners from Berwick could help the defences and the land about, which was waste, could be made profitable. Dacre was granted £220 for the repairs to be carried out. The Earl of Surrey was impressed by the defences. Even if the outer ward were taken, the keep was "the strongest thing I have ever seen". (1523)

The walls were hit by Albany's guns across the river, but the fortress held and the attack of Scots and French was beaten off. The problem seems to have been paying a sufficient number of troops for a continuous garrison. Repairs were necessary after the siege, and it was regarded as a royal castle.

John Carr of Hetton was keeper of the Castle from 1538 to his death in 1551. On taking over he found there was much to do — the roof of the keep was half off and the gatehouse and corner tower were in the same condition. Surrey's defence were of earth and stone, needing to be converted into complete walls. Dacre's buildings were in need of repair. The royal commissioners considered the Castle was not so strong as Surrey supposed and was open to mining, but the Scots, they thought, were not expert in such matters. £200 could put the Castle into repair as the chief defence of the area to the west of the Till, and 200 men would be well employed here to defend the English and annoy the Scots. Guns, powder and shot were brought from Berwick. In 1542 an attack was threatened and Carr got money to provide for 50 more men. The Scots, however, attacked in the far west and were defeated at Solway Moss.

For several years expensive repairs were undertaken, and seemed endless, for in 1544 part of the wall near the river fell down. John Carr was not entirely trusted because of his Border connections. A report on the Castle showed that the regular garrison was only 25 horsemen and 9 gunners. 10 men were employed on the watch every night, and there was a mixed collection of guns. By 1545 it was considered to be in a proper state of defence and might be used as the base for an intended attack on Scotland. Carr put in a claim for increased pay. Bowes said of him — "Ever since he came to man's age and especially in these last wars, Carre has been forward in every dangerous enterprise and has spared neither friends nor substance in the king's service. Since the beginning of this war he has twice been sore hurt (once left in the field for dead), has once been taken prisoner and has had two brethren slain and the rest of his brethren and his 2 sons taken prisoners. All on these borders agree that no borderer of any sort has achieved so many great adventures to the King's honour."

Wark Castle was again used in 1547 as the base for another Scottish invasion by the Duke of Somerset. Afterwards it was open to retaliation by the Scots assisted by French, and more damage was done. Sir Robert Bowes reported the outer ward was in great decay and the wall near the river needed repair. He favoured extended fortifications to include the village, and said that a brewhouse and bakehouse should be built to ensure supplies.

In Mary's reign Ralph Carr was allowed to recover the Castle, undertaking to keep it under repair, but only a porter, 2 gunners and 8 soldiers in constant residence; but it seems that a private individual could not accomplish the task, and an official wrote "it is doubtful whether Wark or Norham, belonging to subjects, are worth the expense they occasion the Prince in time of war".

Hence the building of the walls of Berwick to make it the key to the frontier.

It seems that a castle in peace time might be plundered by those who were supposed to keep it in repair, and it tended to suffer from neglect.

"In peace it will be in danger to be stolen & in warre in perill to be wonne" by the enemy, with dishonour to the Crown. It was suggested that Queen Elizabeth should take over Wark and refortify it with a great barbican and stabling for 200 horses. Yet another report said that the walls should be 20 feet high and were crumbling especially overlooking the river. The keep was only 34 feet high with a damaged roof and none of the walls were "flanked".

It shows what damage could be done even by an unsuccessful attack; besides the shattering of walls, great harm could be done to roofs and timbers. Lead especially could be damaged. Little wonder that a parsimonious queen was reluctant to carry out repairs. Even so, negotiations were made with Sir Ralph Carr, who lived at Chillingham, to take over the property. But no deal could be made, and it was reported that Wark was "evilly kept . . . . used more like a farm than a place of strength".

Though garrison charges to the Crown were more than £60 a year

"Sir Ralph Grey does nothing at Wark, but suffer it to decay".

There were occasional alerts and extra men sent there, but the decline of the Castle continued.

In 1580 some of the buildings were so shaky that

"no man dare dwell in them & if speedy remedy be not had, they will fall flatte to the ground."

Work was carried out on the site, and in 1592 Sir Ralph Grey wrote that he

"had finished the water wall, save a little in the basement and had enough stone, timber and other materials to finish the work."

Under the Stuarts it was allowed to decay and in 1639, at the time of the Bishops' Wark it was declared worse than useless for defensive purposes. A Scottish force, however, used it in 1644 when on the way to assist the Parliamentary army.

In spite of neglect and decay in 1863 a lot of the Castle was still standing — several hundred yards of wall and the S.W. tower or keep. Some walls were demolished as dangerous.

The donjon was multangular in shape and measured roughly 85 yards by 55 yards. Two lower storeys were recognizable, and a flight of stone steps led down to the inner ward. The wall separating the inner and outer baileys was still visible. The west and east walls could also be traced. There was a "secret" tunnel — a sewer leading from inside the Castle to the river. This, on one occasion, was used by English troops to recover the Castle from the Scots. They knew the hidden way. Time has continued to have its effect on the site, which becomes both eroded and overgrown.

Perhaps some day English Heritage will take over and conduct excavations to uncover a site, which was one of the earliest motte and bailey castles, and witnessed more than 500 years of Border warfare.

Castle Heaton

Turning eastwards from Wark and below Twizell was Heton Castle, defended on one side by the River Till. In 1541 the town of Heaton where

"standeth the ruinous walls of an old castle lykwyse rased & casten downe by the king of Scottes . . . . A great part of the vawtes & walls of the said castell be yet standing without any ruffes or flores."

It had belonged in 1415 to Sir Thomas Gray and was listed as a "Castle". A plan of it in the reign of Elizabeth shows it still, though ruinous, as an extensive set of buildings in a quadrangular enclosure with curtain walls and four corner towers like Ford and Chillingham. It was then considered suitable for restoration and could receive a garrison of 300 horsemen.

"This Castell of Heton haithe bene a pleasaunt & beautiful building, in manner square, with goodlie Towers & Turrettes, as is yett remaininge, the Lyons tower on the west side thairof the southe coyne of Corner & on the northe sydeor pairte one mansion of a vawte that a 100 horse may stand in & a number of shelles & welles that haithe been glorious buildings & housinge, now ruinous & alle in decaie."

On one tower was a large carving of a lion rampant, the emblem of the Hetons and the Greys. The site is now a farmstead, and most of the old buildings have disappeared. However, at one side of the modern cattleyard is a long stone building with a vaulted basement. It is something like 70 feet long and 17 feet wide. There are projecting stone stairs that look into the cattleyard and the upper floor is a loft. The vaulted basement may well have been part of the accommodation for 100 horses. Wallis mentions that two wells were discovered, and from them were taken four pewter plates with the arms of Grey upon them.

Heton (or Heaton) is said to be ghosted (Grey or Gray).

Two miles along the River Till and on the eastern side of it, are the remains of **Etal Castle,** overlooking the site of former bridge, ford and ferry. Etal belonged to the barony of Muschamp and was leased by the Manners family, who were usually "Roberts" by name. After William Heron of Ford got a licence to "crenellate" his mansion in 1338, Robert Manners retaliated in 1341 by similarly fortifying his home, which was afterwards called a castle. Another Robert held it in 1415 and in 1449 we find yet another Robert leasing the lands of Howtell under the title of "Robert Maners of Etekk lord of that ilke".

Another Manners married into the Roos family and his son became Lord Roos. His son, Thomas, in 1525 became Earl of Rutland. Obviously Etal was no longer their residence and the Castle was kept by a constable, usually a Collingwood.

In 1513 Etal Castle was taken by James and suffered damage, and in 1533 the Scots devastated New Etal on the other side of the river. The 1541 report said that there was no fortress at New Etal and inhabitants had to resort to the castle. The bridge over the Till collapsed in 1541 and until then "allwanis redy passage over when the said river is waxen greate & past rydynge upon horsebacke."

In 1535 Henry Collingwood, a "sharp borderer" was there with 30 horsemen.

An exchange was made with the Crown, which enabled the King to take over the Castle. It was said to be capable of accommodating 100 men. But the Crown did not effect repairs, and in 1564 "the queen's house at Etal is greatly decayed, scant able to lodge the captain".

In 1604 the Etal estate consisted of some 2,000 acres with 29 houses, 2 wauk mills, 2 corn mills and a dovecote. James I gave it to George Hume, who became Earl of Dunbar. Then it was held by Lord Theophilus Howard, who sold it to Robert Carr, one of the many Scots who benefitted from the coming of a Stuart King. Previously they belonged to the raiders, and two Carrs of Kerrs of Cessford became Earls in England.

Etal Castle was important in a chain of defences, and the Manners family held a number of places, including Branxton, Berrington, Buckton and Hethpool, which had towers. It is now maintained by English Heritage and situated in a pleasant estate village. Thatched houses here are a reminder of what was once common roofing.

The river Till closely skirts the north and west sides of the Castle, and the keep house in the north west corner overlooks the site and the river crossing. There is a roughly rectangular enclosure measuring 200 feet from East to West and 180 feet from North to South. The north and east walls have disappeared, but have been traced. There may have been a tower at the N.E. corner. The gatehouse is at the S.E. corner, and the south wall remains to rampart level. There seems to have been a turret halfway along and another at the S.W. corner. There were no doubt other buildings.

The gatehouse is quite impressive, and is about 36 feet square. The entrance is deeply recessed and covered by two towers. The arms of Manners greeted the visitor, still in place above the gate which was reinforced by a portcullis. It is likely that there was a drawbridge, but the ditch has been filled. A doorway at a higher level may indicate an outbuilding or a projecting rampart walk. The entrance passage is vaulted with guard chambers on either side. The upper floor is reached by stone stairs in the north wall; and measures 22 feet by 19 feet. The windows had seats, and in the S.E. corner is a small room, while the N.E. corner has spiral stairs to the roof and a latrine. None of the battlements are left.

The tower house is a four storeyed building with a frontal extension for the entrance, so that it measures 60 feet by 35 feet.

The fore-building had a portcullis and the basement thick walls with a vaulted roof. Higher the walls were not so thick so that the room space was larger. They were reached by spiral stairs on the north side of the entrance. The garderobe was situated in the N.E. angle. Each floor level above the base has windows, and also mural chambers. There was a room at each level in the forebuilding, but this has been reduced almost to foundation level. The spiral stair went up to a square tower, above the battlements which no longer exist. The stonework of the Hall tower is very fine, and it is considered that this was constructed before the gatehouse and the licence to crenellate.

Ford

Next in line along the Till is **Ford Castle,** originally the abode of the Herons. It was from 1338 that their house became a castle. They had other lands and were connected with Chipchase by marriage. William Heron was listed as the owner of Ford Castle in 1415. A younger William Heron was killed in an attack on Etal in 1428, and this led to a family feud. The priors of Tynemouth and Durham in arbitration ruled that John Manners should have 500 masses sung for the repose of William Heron and pay his widow 250 marks. There was also a dispute about the wardship of his son, and the King took over for a time. The Castle had been reduced to ruins by the feud. John Heron, the son, married a kinswoman and was employed by the Crown to search into the smuggling of wool. He was committed to the Lancastrian side, but managed to stay constable of Bamburgh when the Yorkists took over. In 1461 he was killed at Towton fighting for Henry VI.

The lands were forfeited, but recovered by the family soon after, and a William Heron owned Ford Castle at the time of James IV's attack, but was then held hostage in Scotland. His wife was trying to negotiate his release through the Earl of Surrey and not philandering with the Scottish King as some have imagined. After Flodden her husband was exchanged for George Hume.

In 1541 Ford was said to be burnt by the King of the Scots in 1513, and although some repairs had been done "the great buildinges & most necessarye houses restech ever sythens waste & in decay."

Restored it could house a hundred horsemen and more for Border service. There was some trouble about the possession of Ford. The heiress had married Thomas Carr, and the Herons of Chipchase claimed the property. Thomas Carr was expelled, but his supporters attacked the Herons, and Giles Heron died of wounds. In 1558 Thomas Carr was murdered, and the feud continued for many years. His son William was a minor under wardship of the Crown, and the estate continued to provide disputes within the family. In 1661 Thomas Carr was killed by his stepfather, John Radcliffe, and the estate was disputed by heiresses.

Francis Blake, husband of Elizabeth Carr, began to buy up lands of the others. Later in his will, he made his grandson Francis Delaval his heir, and the provision for his wife gives some idea of Ford Castle. She was to have the dining room, the silk room, the room in which she lay and the room above it with the kitchen above the stairs and the cellar beneath. She was allowed to use the brewhouse under the tower and the tower house and the rooms belonging to it. She could have produce from the gardens, pigeons from the dovecote, rabbits from the warren and coal from the colliery. She could also use the stables under the east tower. This gives some idea of the extent of the Castle when Francis Delaval took over in 1743.

It was held by the Delavals till 1808 when Lord Delaval died. Then Lady Waterford had the estate till 1827, followed by her son, Marquess of Waterford. His wife later presided over the estate, which was purchased by Lord Joicey in 1907.

The original crenellated manor house had a high walled enclosure. It suffered attacks from the Scots and the Manners of Etal. In 1513 the Castle suffered and again in 1547, when only one tower was left to shelter the garrison. Some idea of the extent of the Castle can be obtained from the time of Francis Blake, when having acquired the whole property he began to make alterations.

The Castle was quadrangular with corner towers. The biggest is the N.W. now called the King James Tower, and the west gateway was beneath it and another building to the south. A strong curtain wall connected it with the S.W. tower, which also stands. The curtain wall crosses to the east tower, used as stabling. (see above). The wall continues north to a large rectangular building or hall shown as "old" on the plans. Its long axis is north to south. Between this and the James Tower, new buildings were constructed for Sir Francis Blake.

The plan shows a two storey building with attics above and cellars below. Steps to the main entrance show that the main floor is above ground level and the cellars partly below. There seems to be corner towers at each end connected with the older buildings. The outer court was converted into a garden area. The Delavals pushed out the enclosure to take this within the walls, and constructed the ornamental Gothic gateway with false portcullis and gun ports that still stands. They removed the curtain walls and the east tower. Further landscaping took place. To the north of the Castle is a very deep ravine with a stream that provided protection for it.

The old village of Ford lay to the west of the Castle, where mounds indicate the lines of old houses. The vicar's pele, with its vaulted basement, still stands to first floor level. It was capped by Lady Waterford because it spoilt the view; and the village was removed to another site to the east of the Castle and respectfully away from it.

Lady Waterford, who was an admirer of Sir Walter Scott, restored some of the more medieval features of the Castle and maintained the adjacent Church. Ford Castle is not open to the public, but it can be viewed from the road, the churchyard and the fields. In springtime the area is glorious with daffodils; and another attraction is the Lady Waterford Hall, formerly the village school, decorated by Lady Waterford's own wall paintings.

Duddo

In 1541 at Grindonrigg was a little tower of John Selby, kept in good repair, and only half a mile from **DUDDO.**

North of Etal on a rocky crag 300 feet above sea level and overlooking the countryside is what appears to be a giant monolith, and one wonders whether some romantic fashioner of the landscape was trying to establish a connection with the Five Stones of Duddo, a prehistoric monument. But in 1541 it is reported

"At Duddo there standeth a pece of a tower that was rased and casten down by the King of Scotts in the said warre 40 yeres since . . ."

It belonged to the Claverings and the war was in 1496.

In Bates's Border Holds 1888 there is a photograph of much of the tower still standing after restoration. It was roughly 36 feet square but on the south side was a stair turret projecting 10 feet and measuring $13\frac{1}{2}$ feet across. Its east wall contained the entrance, and above it was a corbelled turret, which was entered at third floor level. It seems to have had a barmkin, and the rebuilding took place after 1561.

The stair turret seems to have been characteristic of this period as indicated by the so called "bastle" of Doddington. William Clavering of Duddo died in 1586, mortally wounded in a skirmish with the Scots. The photograph of 1888 shows that the northern wall had crumbled and the stair turret was split from top to bottom. Raine, in his North Durham, described a large barn near the tower, which was removed about 1850.

Mackenzie, in 1825, wrote of the tower —

"A vault, which has been a safe hold for cattle, forms the principal remains."

He gave the number of Duddo Stones as six, and people considered them to be a monument of yet another battle with the Scots. James IV and his army would have noticed these and the ruined tower on the way to attack Etal and Ford Castles in 1513, before defeat and death at Flodden.

Fenton is two miles S.E. of Ford and was one of the more important secondary defences in 1415. It could garrison 40 men, and in 1541 it was "a grett towre with a barmekyn with other necessary houses within the same".

In 1542 it was regarded as a "house of strengthe" along with Etal and Ford. One hundred foot soldiers were here in 1549 under Sir John Forster and Scottish prisoners were housed here for a time. Fenton tower has disappeared from history beneath a large farmstead.

Howtell is three miles S.W. of Ford, overlooking Beaumont Water with Kilham on the other side, where a tower was built after 1541. At that time Howtell, though attacked by the king of Scots, still had a great part of the walls standing and could be repaired.

It was not a place of primary importance, and about the size of Hethpool which was beyond Kilham. Howtell tower stands among farm buildings and measures 33 feet by 31 feet. The stonework is rough except the quoins, and the walls are 6½ feet in thickness with entrance on the south. It is not possible to say whether it had a vaulted basement and a timber floor is more likely.

Hethpool is situated in hill country, much inhabited in prehistoric times and in medieval times until some retreat was necessary from natural forces and raiders.

In 1342 it was "for the most part devastated by the Scots, rebels and enemies of the King". It suffered again in 1385 and 1399, but a tower had been built by 1415.

In 1541 it was "a lytle stone house or pyle which ys a great releyffe to the tenants thereof."

Hethpool was not considered as one of the ring of fortresses. It was a small square tower, which has been mostly dismantled. One wall provides a romantic ivy-clad ruin at the end of the garden of the modern house. Collingwoods once held the property here, and Admiral Collingwood planted acorns to provide for future "wooden walls" that ruled the sea. It is an attractive area, sparsely inhabited. Wild goats haunt the upper crags.

Kilham, a neighbouring settlement and similarly ransacked by raiders, was described in 1541 as having no tower, barmkin or place of refuge. Yet it was said to be a suitable place for housing a number of soldiers. The trouble seems to have been the work of reivers rather than any official force. Raiders were able to strike down as far as Wooler. The Storeys were a surname in this area and by 1584 a tower seems to have been built. It is said to have had no great strength and was similar to the bastle house at **Doddington.** This still stands in a ruinous condition and it was evidently neither a tower nor the type of bastle described in the recent H.M.S.O. survey. It might be described as a country house built in the old style.

Nesbit is very near to Doddington, and in 1415 there was a tower belonging to Sir Thomas Grey. In 1541 the tower "is longe synce for lack of reparacons decayed & fallen & no fortresse there now remayneth". This might explain the construction of the bastle at Doddington.

Doddington Bastle

Detailed plans of this made in 1986-7 were included in the 14th volume of the County History.

The building measures 60 feet by 25 feet. It has a projecting porch, and stair turret on the south side. Originally it was three storeys high with an embattled parapet and a steeply sloping roof. The windows were small, seemingly 4 on each long side for each floor. The walls were not massive and sufficiently strong for the size of the building, so that they had to be re-inforced by thickening inside and buttresses outside. All the floors were wooden and there was no vaulted basement. The circular stone stair rose to roof level and a stone in the north parapet carried the date of the building as 1584 by Sir Thomas Grey of Chillingham and Wark. He was one of the commissioners who made a survey of castle and towers between Berwick and Harbottle in this same year. Doddington was not included, so was it not regarded as a tower? Four centuries later it is in a roofless, ruinous condition, inhabited by birds and trees. Only the stair turret stands high — Whitton Shields, near Morpeth, gives a very good idea of what it was like when inhabited.

Barmoor is situated on the Berwick road, north of Doddington. It belonged to the Muschamp barony and had a tower. In 1541 we have

"at byermore . . . . there ys a tower. of the inheritance of Mr. Muschyens in extreme decay & almost ruinous for lack of reparacions."

It seems to have had some repairs for on a chimney piece was cut the date 1584 with the initial M for Muschamp. Another stone tells of later owners — William Carr of Etal and his wife Margaret   being the evidence.

In 1801 Barmoor was rebuilt in castle style by John Patterson of Edinburgh for the Sitwells. An old porch and some of the walls of the old tower were embodied in the building.

Lowick, a mile eastwards, was situated on the Roman Road called Devil's Causeway, which was much used in medieval times.

In 1541 there was tower belonging to Mr. Swinburne. In 1584 Commissioners considered it as well worth repair as "these upon the ring of the border".

But no more is heard of the tower and it may be recorded by the term 'Bastle corner' on Lowick Hall Farm.

Still further eastwards on a hill is **East Kyloe,** where there was a tower belonging to the Greys. It was inhabited till 1633 and has since become embodied in the farm buildings. The upper storey has gone, but a vaulted basement could be detected. The walls were 8 feet thick, and the tower measured 39 feet by 32 feet with entrance on the south side.

Near the sea and opposite Holy Island is the site of

Fenham Castle. It has been recorded as a motte and bailey castle. The mound and the ramparts of the bailey can still be traced in a field south of the farm.

Nothing is recorded about it, but it was used in the Civil War and was captured from the Scots and Royalists by Colonel Fenwick, who was Governor of Berwick in 1651. There was a mill and granary near, and there used to be boat connections with Holy Island. There was a manor house at Fenham which belonged to the Priory, and Canon Raine reported on the remains in his book on North Durham. The Durham connection causes some complications, and the properties of the Bishop were not recorded in County surveys. A Survey Book of Norham & Islandshire mentions at Fenham

"There is in the same towne one towre in good reparacions".

There were two towers at Elwick and one at Goswick in good repair. Those at Cheswick and Thornton were in ruinous condition.

"In the same town of **Ancroft** is one pile, builded to the end of the church & divers good houses beside."

The tower at Ancroft could be regarded as a Vicar's Pele or a fortified church tower. It was strongly built with a vaulted basement and a spiral stair in the S.E. corner. It has two upper storeys and narrow but widely splayed windows gave sufficient light. The village of Ancroft was much larger in olden times than it is today.

Belford had a castle in 1415, belonging to Lord Darcy. It was on the site of what is now Belford West Farm, and very little of it can be detected. It was said to be moated and this perhaps was not unusual.

For the defence of the coast there was Bamburgh and

"the forte of Beblowe within that **HOLY ISLAND,** which lieth very well for the defence of the haven there."

It was suggested in 1550 that a ring of bulwarks could be constructed and a moat on the landward side. The fort had been built in the reign of Henry VIII and stone from the Priory was used for the purpose. It had a permanent garrison, with gunners and guns. This continued until 1820, when it became a coastguard station.

In 1903 it was purchased by Edward Hudson of Country Life, and restored by the famous architect, Sir Edwin Lutyens, as a modern residence in medieval style. The Castle is now under the care of the National Trust, and can be visited by permission of the tide, which twice by night and day covers the road between the mainland and the Island.

It is an attractive place with a church, ruins of the Priory and the Castle itself. It has a small harbour with fishing and pleasure boats. Sea birds haunt the place, which is associated with Saint Cuthbert, who died on March 20th 687 in his cell on the Farne Islands. He was buried at Lindisfarne, but with Viking attacks on the coast from 793, his coffin was moved. He travelled to various parts of the north country till he finally came to rest at Durham. His coffin is still there and because of his travels, the Bishop of Durham could claim Norham, Islandshire and Bedlingtonshire within the County of Northumberland.

The Castle and Cathedral of Durham are two of the finest works of Norman architecture in the country, and had their influence on the castles and churches of Northumberland.

From Holy Island or Lindisfarne there are magnificent views over the sea and the land. Grandest of all is Bamburgh Castle. Bamburgh, as a Saxon stronghold, was well known to Saint Cuthbert, who visited the royal palace at that place. **Haggerston** manor house was "crenellated" in 1345, and in 1541 it
"was a strong tower in a good state of repair".
In 1618 a fire destroyed a good part of the hall, and the old tower was pulled down in 1805.

Bamburgh

Bamburgh is a most impressive site for a castle, being a rocky outcrop dominating the coast, the sands, the sea and the present day village. It was used in prehistoric and Roman times as a natural fortress. In Anglo-Saxon times it became a 'burgh', established by King Ida about 547 A.D. and called Bebbanburh after a later Queen of Northumbria — "timbered Bebbanburh, that was first with hedge surrounded and thereafter with wall".

At first a royal town, it declined, but William of Normandy saw the importance of the place, to defend the coast and oppose Scottish inroads since the land was claimed by Malcolm Canmore, King of the Scots. Before the end of William's reign there was already a castle on the rock. One duty of tenants was carting timber to the castle, for fortification and fires.

During the rebellion of Robert de Mowbray, Earl of Northumberland in 1095, Bamburgh was held against William II (Rufus). The King besieged the castle and erected against it an opposing wooden fort, called malvoisin (or evil neighbour). The Earl escaped and his wife held the fort till he was captured, and when the King threatened to put out his eyes she surrendered. This incident shows that women could be concerned in military matters.

Later, especially in Stephen's reign, the castle was not held successfully against the Scots, but Henry II asserted his authority. Between 1164 and 1170 the great stone keep was built — similar to Newcastle. It had curtain walls of stone that encircled the summit of the rock, and other buildings included a chapel.

In 1183 the castle and castlegate were repaired, and in 1221 a good grange 150 feet by 34 feet was to be constructed within the walls. Ballisters and other defensive weapons were provided, and the drawbridge was repaired. Accounts show the continual supplies of timber were necessary, and violent gales were a problem, destroying the mills in 1243. Maintained by Edward I, the castle was neglected by Edward II and in Edward III's reign (1330) it was reported that the great tower, other towers, hall, chambers, the grange and gates were in such a state of disrepair that the place would soon be ruinous as well as roofless. A few years later it was sufficiently repaired to defeat a Scottish attack. On occasion it seems constables were not trustworthy, and John de Fenwyk seems to have taken timber, ironwork, lead and even the King's own table for his own use.

Bamburgh played an important part in the Wars of the Roses. It had surrendered to Edward IV, but was recovered by Queen Margaret in 1462. She escaped before it was besieged by the Earl of Warwick, who had an army of 10,000 men. The castle surrendered, but later Sir Ralph Percy let it go again.

In 1464 Warwick came again with big guns and demanded surrender. Sir Ralph Grey, the constable, refused since Bamburgh was considered to be impregnable. Great cannon called 'Newcastle', 'London' and 'Dijon' fired at the walls and stones flew into the sea. The Castle had to surrender and the constable, who was held responsible for the damage, was put to death. Presumably some repairs were made, but in 1538 when Henry VIII considered the defences of the realm many repairs were necessary — a new drawbridge and a new gate for the gate house, $4\frac{1}{2}$ yards high and $3\frac{1}{2}$ yards broad. The walls were in need of repair and roofs. A baulk of timber $6\frac{1}{2}$ yards long could be obtained "from chopewell woods, weste of Newcastle", which belonged to Newminster Abbey. All the timber could be brought by water. Six baulks of timber 8 yards long were needed and 20 tons of other timber from Chopwell. Parts of the Castle were said to be full of sand, presumably blown from the dunes. This emphasises the continual and heavy cost of repairs. But the natural rock still stood high, and Leland at the same time calls Bamburgh "sometime a huge and great castle, one of the strongest in these parts".
William Patten, who was there in 1547 with the Duke of Somerset, wrote —

"The plot of this castle standeth so naturally strong, that hardly can anywhere (in my opinion) be found the like, inaccessible on all sides . . . . . This castle is very ancient and called in Arthur's days (as I have heard) Joyous Garde."

But it was neglected, and in Elizabeth's reign Sir John Forster plundered it and James I, who had no use for it, granted it to Claudius Forster in 1610. The Forsters continued to neglect the property, and in 1704 it was purchased by Lord Crewe, - Bishop of Durham, to pay off the debts. He later married Dorothy Forster, and Thomas Forster was involved in the Jacobite Rebellion of 1715.

The Crewe Trustees undertook the work of restoring the castle. Dr. Sharpe, Archdeacon of Northumberland, in 1769, it was reported

"has repaired and rendered habitable the gret Norman square tower; the part reserved for himself and his family, is a large hall and a few smaller apartments: but the rest of the spacious edifice is allotted for purposes which make the heart to glow with joy when thought of. The upper part is an ample granary, from which corn is dispensed to the poor without distinction . . . Other apartments are fitted up for shipwrecked sailors . . . ."

"Much has been done since his time: and it affords matter of high gratification, to see the venerable fortress gradually reclaimed from ruin and converted into apartments for the most wise and benevolent uses. A large room is fitted up for educating the boys of the neighbourhood, on Dr. Bell's system. A suite of rooms are allotted to two mistresses and 20 poor girls, who from their ninth year are lodged, clothed and educated till they be fit for service. Here too is a market for meal and groceries, which are sold to the poor at prime cost, on Tuesdays and Fridays. Medicines and advice are given at the infirmary on Wednesdays and Saturdays, and in 1810, 1050 out patients were admitted to its benefit and 36 in patients; of whom 34 died, 8 were sent to Newcastle Infirmary and the rest either cured or relieved. Various signals too are made use of to warn vessels in thick and stormy weather, from the rocks of the Farne Islands. A life boat and all kinds of implements useful in saving crews and their vessels in distress, are always in readiness; also beds for shipwrecked sailors: and all means used to prevent vessels being plundered and for restoring them to their owners." (Hodgson).

In this connection Bamburgh will always be associated with the name of the heroine Grace Darling, who died there in 1842. Her grave is in the churchyard opposite to the Grace Darling Museum.

Towards the end of the last century, Bamburgh Castle, again suffering the ravages of time and tide, was purchased by Lord Armstrong and restored by him. He made his fortune from ships and armaments, and it is perhaps fitting that he should restore an ancient castle to its old splendour. It has again become a place of kings when films are made. The great hall is so much like a place that it was used for the BBC Fall of Eagles — the European Empires of Germany, Austria and Russia. In the castle are housed a fine collection of treasures and a special exhibition of Tudor period armour from the Tower of London.

Bamburgh Castle is open to the public in summer months, but a good look before entry is well worth while — to see the nature of the site and to detect the different periods of building. The approach is from the east, but the road is so arranged that the ascent of the slope is under the supervision of the walls and tower up to the gate-house and beyond. The entrance is at a lower level than the summit of the rock, and the road is partly cut from rock. Two towers guard the entrance which would have ditch and drawbridge originally. Beyond the barbican the road into the castle interior is covered by walls and towers above. There is a second gateway to the bailey, which contained the Norman chapel and other buildings. Some medieval walling still remains and it is difficult to determine the extent of restoration. The original entrance was from the west into the west bailey, where the approach and the remains of a barbican and towers have been revealed.

The keep dominates the site. It measures 69 feet by 61 feet, but is fifty five feet in height, considerably less than Newcastle or Norham. This was because the height and strength of the rock made a safe entrance at ground level. It could be very difficult to reach the entrance of the keep. Here again the architecture has been obscured in restoration, and it is not certain how much Dr. Sharpe rebuilt.

The basement is vaulted in 3 chambers, and the largest had a central arcade of 3 arches from which ribs struck to the outer wall and cross wall. The mural galleries are difficult to interpret because of the restoration, but the keep is interesting to explore. On the ramparts old cannons are on display and there are views to Holy Island and the Farnes, over Bamburgh village and the surrounding countryside. Bamburgh has attracted many painters, photographers and writers — it is a 'castle of castles'.

In the **Bamburgh** area a number of towers have disappeared — one at Outchester and another that overlooked Budle harbour. The tower at North Sunderland was demolished in 1790. The Forsters held Adderstone Hall and Beadnell Tower, which was left by Thomas Forster, in 1587, to his son. The building is now readily recognizable as the Craster Arms in Beadnell near to the church.

PRESTON TOWER still stands in part on a hill to the west. It was a rectangular hall with corner towers, but it has been truncated and what remains is the south front with two corner towers. It has been converted into a clock tower for the modern hall and provides both a landscape feature and a viewpoint over the gardens and countryside. It is open to the public in summer months. The building stands 50 feet high. The side walls are $6\frac{1}{2}$ feet thick and the total breadth is 30 feet. The towers are about 13 feet square and have vaulted basements. There are rooms with fireplaces above these.

To the south of Preston is **Embleton,** with a very fine example of a vicar's pele. It was built in 1395 at a cost of £40 after the ravages of the Scots. In the basement are double vaults, and the tower measures 40 feet by 20 feet. It has been altered, and is dwarfed by the later vicarage. The mural staircase has gone, and it is quite likely that the entrance to the first floor was by a door at that height, the churchyard being at a higher level. There is a second floor and a roof walk with battlements. The vicarage was once the abode of Bishop Mandell Creighton, who wrote a History of the Popes. Embleton has a fine church with a medieval tower; and two dovecotes, one medieval of stone and the other eighteenth century of red brick.

Between Embleton and Craster is **Dunstan Hall or Proctor's Stead.** It is medieval in origin and it has been claimed to be the birthplace or abode of Duns Scotus, the celebrated medieval scholar, who gains a place at Wallington Hall among local worthies.

The buildings have changed greatly in time and were last restored by Mr. Honeyman in the 1930s. Of the original building, there remains the east and west towers, between which would have been another building, which was much altered in the seventeenth century and later. The eastern tower was cut in height to fit this, and there was a stair turret added on the north side. The west tower still remains and measures 18 feet by 15 feet, built of large blocks of stone. It stands as the highest part of the building, but the walls have been angled down to the south, to give a stepped effect. A family long connected with Dunstan had the name of Wetwang, and one of these built the towers in the fourteenth century. Henry Wetwang sold the estate in 1690, and it was later acquired by the Proctors, hence the change of name to Proctor's Stead.

ROCK. The village of Rock stands westwards from Embleton and on the other side of the railway, but not as far as the A1 road. It is an estate village with a restored church of Norman origin. The hall at the west end of the village is now used as a Youth Hostel, and is situated in extensive grounds.

It was a place of importance in medieval times and guarded by a strong tower. In 1549 it was used as the headquarters for a band of Spanish mercenary troops under the command of Sir Julian Romero. The Scots were supported at this time by French troops as Border Wars continued.

At Rock Hall on the south side a rectangular tower represents the old structure. It is divided by an inner wall and had a smaller tower on the south side. There was yet another tower about 20 feet square on the north side. A manor house was added on the north side by the Salkelds in the seventeenth century. The house went to ruin after a great fire in 1752. It was restored after 1819 by the Bosanquet family, who still own the estate. A good view of the Hall is obtained from the churchyard. It shows an addition to the south, the rebuilding of the central hall and the northern end not rebuilt.

DUNSTANBURGH is a castle of the fourteenth century and unusual in some ways. It was built for a member of the royal family, the Earl of Lancaster, who at times opposed Edward II. In 1315, a year after Bannockburn, he obtained a licence to crenellate, and constructed a castle of great strength on an exposed coastal headland. Coast castles needed strong defences and the nature of the site was such that it could not be attacked from the sea, though the castle had its own safe anchorage.

The defended area was large — some 11 acres — occupying the whole of the promontory. A wall extended from the northern cliff face to the south, and at each end of it was a square tower: Lilburn's tower above the northern scarp face and the Egyncleugh tower overlooking the sea to the south. In between them arose the great mass of the gatehouse, which dominated the area. It gave access to the smaller ward and the domestic apartments. Two great 80ft. drum towers were the essence of the gatehouse, but there seems to have been some weakness and later, in the time of John Gaunt, this entrance was closed and another constructed to the north with a barbican. So the gatehouse became a keep intended for the use of the Earl himself. There was a special constable's tower to the east, with extra quarters attached. A considerable force could be accommodated within the Castle and under the control of the lord himself.

These were dangerous days with rebellions as well as Scottish invasions to consider. Earl Thomas of Lancaster was, like Edward III later, enchanted by the stories of King Arthur and his Knights. This has given romantic associations to Dunstanburgh, and Sir Thomas Malory refers to castles of the Northumberland coast in his 'Morte d'Arthur'. He fought during the Wars of the Roses, and was imprisoned (1469-70) by Edward IV. His work dates to 1471, when he died; and it was printed by Caxton in 1485.

John Lewyn, mason of Durham, had carried out the improvements for John of Gaunt. The new gatehouse was vaulted, having a barbican, postern and drawbridge. It seems that continuous repairs were necessary, especially during the Wars of the Roses. Queen Margaret was there in 1460, since it was a Lancastrian castle. She returned in 1462, and recovered Bamburgh, Dunstanburgh and Alnwick from the Yorkists. Edward IV and Warwick, based at Warkworth, came to recover them. Dunstanburgh surrendered, but Sir Ralph Percy later handed it and Bamburgh back to Henry VI. Both were stormed by the Yorkists in 1464, and great damage was done by cannons. Some repairs were carried out, but in the reign of Henry VIII the donjon and towers needed reroofing, and it was reported that timber could be obtained from Chopwell for beams and floors. The walls also needed attention, and there was "no horse mylne in the said castell".

Similar reports continue throughout the Tudor period, and it does not seem that repairs were effectively carried out. That the towers still stand so high, 500 years after the end of the Wars of the Roses, indicates the strength of the masonry. The curtain walls have suffered a great deal from stone robbers.

Dunstanburgh, in its splendid decay, attracted artists, and in particular Turner, who liked to depict the angry sea. The Castle has its moods: when the waves crash in the Rumbling Churn and the spume flies, it is a reminder of the roar of the cannons in the wars. On the other hand there is a no more delightful walk on a sunny day than along the stretch of turf from Craster to Dunstanburgh, with the smell of the sea and the sight of so many sea-birds. It can be very lonely and it can attract long trails of visitors. It is now under the care of English Heritage and well worth visiting.

Since Dunstanburgh was not restored as a residence like some castles, it is possible to study the military architecture of the building. The site is some 100 feet above sea level. From the south the great drum towers are most impressive, and even more so when standing 80 feet high. They are 105 feet in width, rounded to the front and squared to the rear. The frontal curves project 16 feet outwards from a gateway 11 feet wide, and the tunnel entrance extends 40 feet to the inner court. It would have had gates and portcullis with guard chambers on either side. In the John of Gaunt period both ends were blocked and the flanking towers were entered from doors to the spiral stairs on the N.E. and N.W. The lower floor was used for stores with a dungeon underneath, and the floors above provided apartments and the Great Hall.

The front was carried 2 storeys higher to get the full height. Gaunt's entrance was from the south west with a tower, portcullis and barbican. This was protected by a long battlemented wall called a mantlet. Attackers would be subjected to prolonged fire in this entrance passage. There was also a rock cut moat before the south front, where the walls stand to a considerable height. On the western side much of the masonry has gone, but Lilburn's tower on the N.W. angle still stands to its full height with battlements; and guards the postern gate.

There is a steep rocky descent to the land, and eastwards the sea girt cliffs are only accessible to sea birds.

A number of grass-grown foundations of buildings can be seen to the south of the Castle, and this may have been a settlement. In 1382 six houses were constructed. Dunstanburgh was a part of the barony of Embleton, and the Castle can be approached from the village of that name. The sands of Embleton are a contrast to the rocks of Dunstanburgh.

South of Dunstanburgh and also outside the defensive ring is **Craster**, belonging to one of the oldest families in the country. They consider Percies to be latecomers.

Situated on high ground overlooking the coast is Craster Tower, which was there in 1415. It is strongly built of local stone and rectangular in shape, measuring 35 feet by 30 feet. The entrance was on the east side, and it had a spiral stair, which has been blocked by later building. The vaulted basement is 16 feet across and reaches a height of 10 feet at the apex. It had slits for lighting and ventilation. The upper floors have received more modern windows, and the battlements have been rebuilt. Like Embleton Pele, the basement was used for storage purposes in modern times, since the temperature remains low and unchangeable.

A fine eighteenth century Georgian house has been added to the tower, and there is a high battlemented wall with a gatehouse passage across the road.

Howick, further south along the coast, also had a tower, but this was pulled down about 1780 to make way for the rebuilding of the Hall, which was perhaps then attached to it. Both Craster and Howick had prehistoric fortifications.

Little Houghton, to the west, also had a medieval tower which has been much built about. It measured 30 feet by 25 feet, with walls five feet thick. The basement was vaulted and it had a spiral staircase.
George Mark, in 1734, wrote that the building was "remarkable as a strong tower of great antiquity".
It belonged to the Roddam family, and a fireplace has the date 1674 with the initials E.R.M.-Edward and Mary Roddam.

To the west on the A1, north of Alnwick, is **Hefferlaw Tower,** situated on high ground with views of the countryside. It was a notorious place for travellers on the old road, but it has now been bypassed and can be visited. It was probably an outpost for Alnwick. It measures 24 feet by 30 feet and was 3 storeys high. Some sculptured stones in the building indicate connections with both Alnwick Abbey and the Castle — the crossed croziers of the abbot and the crescent of the Percies.

Northwards on the same road is situated North Charlton. Here is the stump of the village cross in a field called Castle Field. There is a motte or mound which was supposed to be a castle, but the oblong building was a chapel and a graveyard was discovered in the vicinity. The road leads westwards over wild moorland to Hebburn and Chillingham.

Ros Castle is a prehistoric promontory fort, and provides extensive views in all directions with Bamburth and Dunstanburgh prominent. Below it westwards within Chillingham Park stands derelict Hebburn Bastle and Chillingham Castle, restored to occupation. From the same vantage point Chillingham Cattle can be viewed and here I saw the trees come down when "Macbeth" was being filmed on the moor.

Hebburn Bastle is an interesting building and ought to be preserved since it differs from the usual bastles or towers. It has not been altered since the seventeenth century, and stands to roof height with double gables at each end. There are references to it in 1514, 1541 and 1564.
In 1541 it is "a lytle tower of the inheritance of Thomas Hebburne", and in good repair.
In 1564 the owner calls it "my mansion house", and there are indications from a roof line on the south side of another building.

It has been suggested that this was a different building altogether, and that the old tower was pulled down. Experts consider the architecture to be medieval from the style of the masonry and quality of building. It measures about 60 feet by 36 feet, and the walls are very thick, 9 to 10 feet. There is a vaulted basement, with a dividing wall at the east end, making a passage from the entrance. There was a pit 8 feet deep, called a dungeon and a spiral stair leading to the first and second floors. The second floor reaches the attic level with the double roof and windows in each of the gables, which reach a height of 50 feet. There were 3 rooms on the first floor with windows; and two had fireplaces. The largest room was in the middle.

The Hebburn family arms were 3 sable cressets on a silver ground. The cressets were symbols of the beacon, which would be lit on Ros Castle in time of danger, but it presumably refers to 'burn' in the family name. There is the remarkable arbitration by Edmund Craster and Luke Ogle by which a blood feud was ended between the Hebburns and the Storys. The battles in this area nowadays are likely to be those between Chillingham Wild White bulls contending for the leadership of the herd. The old bastle building is well observed from Hepburn Forestry Park. The split in the walls above the entrance was the place of the spiral stair.

Hepburn Bastle

Doddington Bastle, Stair turret stands to full height

Dunstanburgh Castle by the sea

Chillingham Castle

In the thirteenth century there was a manor house, which was sacked by the Scots in 1296. Later in 1344/5 Sir Thomas Heton obtained a licence to fortify his mansion with a wall of stone and lime, and to strengthen it, to crenellate and convert it to a castle. The area was being ravaged by the Scots and much land laid waste. Some parts of the castle already existed but it developed into a rectangular enclosure with a strong tower at each corner, linked by curtain walls.

The entrance was probably on the west side with the great hall on the east side. There were other buildings such as stables built against the walls, and it was reported to be able to provide accommodation for 100 horsemen.

The Greys had obtained possession of Chillingham after Hetons and Herrons in turn, but little change was made. The castle suffered in the rebellion of 1536, but it was held for the King and repaired by Sir Robert Ellerker by 1541, so that it was in good defensive order.

The strength of the corner towers is impressive, yet they must have appeared more formidable before landscaping. To the east of the castle is a deep ravine and burn. The whole area may have been moated with an extra walled area outside the castle. Landscaping has raised the earth level south of the castle to make lawns, and any depression would be filled. The hall was on the south side.

In the reign of Elizabeth changes were made — the entrance was moved to the north where it still is. Improvements continued in the time of James I, and changes on the south side of the courtyard are attributed to Inigo Jones. This consisted of an arcade with a projecting stone stair, on either side of which were arranged seven of the Nine Worthies. Those identified have been Charlemagne, Godfrey de Bouillon, King Arthur, Hector of Troy, Alexander and Julius Caesar. Three religious figures, not identified, were David, Joshua and Judas Maccabeus.

A grander entrance developed on the north side — a three storied frontispiece with coupled columns, like an Oxford college. Within, on the north side was the long gallery, and other developments made it less military. Lord Grey supported Parliament in the Civil War, and so there was no Cromwellian destruction of the castle. Unlike Ford, later developments did not involve the destruction of any medieval towers at Chillingham, and so it is a particularly good example of its type.

Chillingham Church is close to the Castle, and should be visited, since it contains the finest medieval monument in the county; to Sir Ralph Grey, who died in 1443, and his wife.
Their alabaster figures repose on an alabaster slab above an elaborately decorated tomb chest. There are indications that the whole was coloured, since some fragments of painting remain. Sir Ralph is carved in full plate mail with helmet and equipment, his feet resting on a lion. His wife has the dress and ornament of the time, entirely civilian. Angels are depicted carrying their souls heavenward, while a series of saints and angels are depicted or carved about the tomb chest. They have a freshness and beauty that can be closely admired, since the old railings that surrounded the tomb have been removed.

In 1541 **Chatton,** a mile to the north of Chillingham and belonging to the Earl of Northumberland, had two towers, one of Richard Fowberry and the other of the vicar. Both have disappeared, and very little is left of Coldmartin, south of Wooler. Richard Fowberry had a tower in good repair at Fowberry. This was converted into a comfortable residence in the seventeenth century, and again later, though still called Fowberry Tower.

Further north on Devil's Causeway was Horton Castle, which has disappeared, except for a mound near West Horton Farm. It was in the list of 1415 as 'Horton in Glendale', and again in 1541 as "a great tower with a barmkyne of Sir Roger Graye's inheritance & his chief house in great decay."
This was a great pity since it was so suitable for the defence of the country. Buck has a very fine print of it in 1728 with decay evident — vegetation grows from all the walls. It is sometimes confused with Horton Castle near Blyth (Horton Iuxta Mare) which has also disappeared.

Wooler is the market town of Glendale, an area where there is a confluence of waters; Wooler water, Rivers Glen and Breamish merging into the Till, which makes for the Tweed. This must have caused difficulties of communications and controlled the direction of raids. Wooler was in the direct line of the route along the valley of the Bowmont and Glen. In

Chillingham Castle

Ruins of Wooler Tower

Clennell Hall

Norman times it was the head of the barony of Muschamp, and for this reason had an early castle, probably dating from about 1100.

Its high mound remains in a position dominating the town and the hill has steep slopes. The early castle fell into ruin because of the absence of its lords. In 1254 it was described as of no great value, "being only a waste motte". Wooler itself thrived as a town and was concerned in the wool trade, as well as cattle and sheep markets.

It is not known when the timber fortress was replaced by stone. The present ruins belong to the strong tower built by Sir Thomas Grey of Chillingham in the fifteenth century. It was capable of holding 20 horsemen, and in 1526 there is reference to "the new castle of Wooler". In 1541 though "it stood in a marvellous convenient place for the defence of the country thereabout", half of it was fallen for lack of repair. It seems to have gradually fallen into ruin.

Today there are great masses of masonry on top of the hill. One huge corner has been toppled, another piece lies flat and some stone has fallen down the hillside. A weakness may have been the type of stonework, including large granite blocks or boulders, not shaped because of hardness.

Appropriately a modern war memorial has been set upon the mound that was a castle. It is worth a visit, because from this vantage point Wooler can be surveyed and the hills beyond. It is possible to think of the other defended places of the area — the bastle house at Erle, two stone houses or bastles at Middleton Hall, and an old tower at Lanton, which was cast down by the Scots. There was a tower at Weetwood;

Holborn had a tower with barmkin and Hazelrigg—

"a low tower not finished" by Thomas Haggerston. This was in 1541, when there was no place of refuge at Coupland, but Akeld

"hath in it a little fortlet or bastle house without a barmkin".

AKELD

This has fortunately survived and stands below the hill of its name, and is used for farm purposes. It measures 60 feet by 25 feet and is tunnel vaulted. The base was and still is used for keeping animals.

The loft above provided the accommodation for people in the past. The upper parts have been rebuilt, and the building has been re-roofed, but the basement is of the original stonework. The stone steps at one end are a modern addition. The building is much larger than those in the H.M.S.O. survey and earlier in time.

To the west of Akeld is Yeavering, where an old farm building contains the remains of the old tower. On the top of Yeavering Bell are the ramparts of an Iron Age Hillfort, and below on the plain are the buried foundations of King Edwin's Palace.

Kirknewton Church to the west has the interest that its medieval chancel was built "with pointed tunnel vaults starting so low in the transept that there is no vertical wall at all and in the chancel so little that the small windows from penetrations into the vault". In other words, it is just like the basement of a border tower.

Over the water there was no **Coupland Tower** in 1541, but now there stands a substantial Castle, partly built in medieval style which was L shaped and has battlements. The earliest dating evidence is 1619 carved on the chimney piece of the 'great chamber' with the initials G W & M W. The surname was Wallis, which first appears in connection with Coupland in 1563. The tower of the Castle is 3 storeys high and measures 47 feet by 29 feet. There is a projection on the south side which rises higher and carries the entrance and the staircase. The circular stone stair is 10 feet in diameter, and the basement, with a stone barrel vault, is 36 feet by 18½ feet, giving walls of 5½ feet in thickness. Later divisions were put in, and the great chamber is above. At this floor the spiral stair ends, and three small rooms have been inserted above at different levels. There is a gabled roof and a parapet on corbels with a walk all round. In the early nineteenth century a Tudor style house was added.

South of Wooler is **Lilburn Tower,** which is a nineteenth century mansion designed by Dobson. In 1541 there were 2 towers, one belonging to Cuthbert Proctor, which had fallen into decay and only the walls were standing. The other, which belonged to Sir Cuthbert Ogle, had suffered from a fire. It was said that they should be restored for the defence of the country, and in time of war they could house 100 men. The ruins of the old tower can be seen on a mound near the drive leading down to the present Lilburn Tower. Near it is a ruined medieval chapel, where was found the gravestone 7½ feet long carrying the name 'Alexander', thought to be a Scottish noble who fell in battle. He was carved in full armour with equipment and a dog ornament.

Further south and west of the road was **Ilderton,** which in 1541 had a great tower with a barmkin of stone. But it had fallen into decay and 'should be repaired for it could house 50 men in time of need'. In 1715 it is described as "a mean edifice at present, ye tower, which was ye mansion house, being in ruins."

It has disappeared and so has **Bewick** tower, which in 1541 was capable of accommodating 50 men in wartime. **Roddam** tower, which had no barmkin, was also decayed, and has gone.

Crawley Tower standing high over Powburn and the Wooler road was then the property of the Herons and in great decay, but it has survived today in part, and has a farmhouse built inside it. Its present appearance seems deliberately designed to be a "folly", but it is old material converted. The south and west walls and part of the east wall stand high, and are 10 feet in thickness. The N.E. corner and part of the north wall have disappeared. The building has been converted into L shape whereas it was rectangular. Licence to crenellate was granted in 1343, and it was very strongly built. The N.E. corner carried the spiral stair to the upper floors. From the surviving south and west walls it measured 50 feet by 36 feet, and was presumably barrel vaulted. It stands some 230 feet above the Breamish in a strongly defensive position on a site which carried very substantial early earthworks, which are probably pre-Roman.

In 1340 John, son of Sir Roger Heron of Ford, lived there, and to it returned after 1513 John, the Bastard Heron, who had been outlawed for his part in killing a Carr of Cessford and gained a pardon for heroic display of Flodden Field, though wounded. We should say he "was mentioned in despatches" and received a reward of £20 from Henry VIII.

Westwards in the Breamish valley at **Ingram** was a little tower in decay that was the parsonage, but this has gone like the one at Whittingham.

However, **Whittingham's** other tower still survives, although in a very shaky condition. In 1415 it belonged to William Heron, and in 1541 to Robert Collingwood, fit for a garrison of 40 horsemen. It measures 42 feet by 36 feet, and the original entrance was on the south side with the spiral stair in the S.E. corner. The basement was barrel vaulted. The original flat roof, with crenellated parapet, was replaced by a double gabled roof as at Hebburn.

In 1845 it was altered by Lady Ravensworth. The battlements were built up with a watch tower on the N.E. corner. The inscription is strange reading today—

"this tower, which was formerly used by the villagers as a place of refuge in time of rapine & insecurity was repaired & otherwise embellished for the use & benefit of the deserving poor. A.D. 1845."

The tower is badly in need of repair, the nineteenth superstructure pressing down on the medieval stonework, which is quite distinct and cracking.

Whittingham was situated at the crossroads of communications from Roman times, being near Devil's Causeway, which ran from Corbridge to Berwick; and a branch road from Learchild linked this road with Dere Street, the main road from York to Edinburgh.

Eslington, two miles west of Whittingham, had a tower in 1415 held by Thomas of Hazlerigg, and in 1514 it was suitable for a garrison of 20 men.

In 1541 there was a tower with barmkin occupied by Robert Collingwood. It was attacked by the Scots in 1587 and severely damaged. Nothing now remains of the old tower, nor at **Great Ryle,** where Thomas Collingwood had built a tower in 1541 and hoped to add a barmkin.

Thomas Alder had built a tower at Prendwick in 1541, but this has gone. The one at **Little Ryle** has survived, embodied in a farmhouse. It is sometimes called a bastle and had a vaulted ground floor. A Tudor doorway and blocked windows can be detected. It measures 57 feet by 25 feet, and has no sign of fortification. Not mentioned in 1541, it is likely to have been built by the Collingwood family shortly afterwards. It seems to have had a staircase turret on the north side, where the blocked door is. The walls are 5 feet thick built of large coursed masonry. It stands on a hill, and its style shows it to be superior to the ordinary bastle.

Callaly Castle is a large country house in beautifully wooded countryside. It is not now open to the public since it is being converted into multiple apartments. It can be viewed by walking up the path to Castle Hill, where there is a prehistoric promontory fort. A story is told that in medieval times, the lord wanted to build his castle here, but his lady did not like the place and schemed to get it pulled down in the night. The Castle was then built on Shepherd's Law, where it still stands as part of the country house — the S.W. corner.

It measured 50 feet by 39 feet, and had a spiral staircase. the basement was vaulted and additions were made to the tower. After the Civil War, it was largely rebuilt by the Claverings: the south front is most attractive. Wings were added later and extensions made so that it became a very large country house — too big to maintain; hence the changes of today.

Screnwood had a tower, and in 1895 D. D. Dixon wrote in his "Whittingham Vale" —

"that some years ago the ruins of a large house with walls of great thickness, having pointed doorways and mullioned windows besides other old foundations, were standing in the green fields east of the present Screnwood House. It is very probable that these were the remains of the border tower and barmekyn of the Horsleys".

The ring of defences continues round the foothills of the Cheviot, where travelling was difficult and pastures were for summer only.

ALNHAM

Alnham is situated in the foothills of the Cheviots at a distance of five miles from the Scottish Border. The old Salters' Road passes through the village, which can be viewed from the ramparts of Castle Hill, a prehistoric hill fort. There are splendid views across country to the coast. The village today is much shrunken — but the ancient church and old rectory make it very attractive, with a stream flowing by. The medieval tower was situated on a mound across the stream from the church.

This tower existed in 1415 and so did the Vicar's Tower, which had a vaulted basement. In 1541 we read "At Alname be two lytle toures whereof the one is the mansion of the vycaredge and the'other of the Inherytaunce of the Kinges majesty p'cell of the Erle of Northuberland's landes, being scarcely in good reparacions".

In 1532 the Earl had complained that some 300 Scots had "brunte a toune of mine called Alenam on Thursday being the 10th of October with all the corne, hay & householde stuff in the said toune and also a woman".

In 1566 there is a further report by the Earl's agent, which shows how properties could be treated by tenants. "Alnham. The lorde hath there a faire stronge Tower of ancient tyme builded & strongly vaulted over & Gates & Dores be all of great strong Iron Barres & a good demayne adjoining thereto, the house is now ruinous & in some decay by reason the farmer useth to carry his sheep up the stares & to lay them in the Chambers, which rotted the vaults & will in short time be the utter decay of the same house if other reformation be not had."

It seems that repairs were not carried out and the Tower has disappeared.

The vicar's pele also became ruinous and the vicar lived elsewhere. At one time it was a fine building with a vaulted basement and walls 9 feet thick. In 1821 John Hodgson made a sketch of it and described the tower as "low and squat".

Later in the century it was restored in such a way that the older parts were obscured. It had a fine walled garden instead of a barmkin. The church was also rebuilt, and the Duke of Northumberland as patron played an important part.

At one time Alnham was famous for the sport of cockfighting, and the champion called "Wellington" defeated appropriately an opponent called "Napoleon".

Alwinton is one of a number of villages close to the Scottish Border that suffered decline in the later Middle Ages; the result of an agricultural recession and Border warfare. Under the shadow of Harbottle Castle there was no need for large fortifications, and in 1541 "At Allayton is a little bastell house of stone, the mansion of the vycaredge scarcely in good repac'ons."

Crawley Tower

Whittingham Tower

Biddlestone Tower, now a chapel

A number of old routes converged on Alwinton, including Clennell Street.

At **Barrow,** very near, was a tower at which in 1522 John Barrow kept 20 men for border service. But it was taken and burnt, so that in 1541

"At Barrow a lytle above Harbottel on the south syde of the same ryver of Cokett standeth the old walls of a lytle fortresse of the inherance of one Gerald Barrowe which in tyme past was brounte & razed by the Scottes in a warre tyme. And so remaineth still waste because the oweners thereof have bene but poor men and not able nor of power sythens to reparell the same."

So it has disappeared like the old vicar's pele. The same fate has befallen Burradon tower. In 1541 it was called a great tower which had fallen into ruin and decay.

Surprisingly the tower at **Biddlestone** has survived in a strange way — converted into a chapel. In 1541 there was a tower and barmkin beloning to Percival Selby which was in good repair, and so was their other little tower at Cotewalls.

At **BIDDLESTONE** a mansion was added to the tower and further buildings later, so that Warburton (1715) wrote — "The east of the house is an old tower; on ye west side of which is added a double wing, a small court on ye south and a handsome gateway."

This hall was supposed to have been the model for "Osbaldistone Hall" in Rob Roy, and the Selbys, who were strong Catholics, would fit into the picture. To this was added yet another building in severe classical style. However, all this has gone, and only the tower survives as the basis for the Catholic chapel. It measures 40 feet by 33 feet, and is barrel vaulted in the basement.

The old trees have gone and modern conifers cluster around like ancient armies.

To the north in the hillside is a deep red gash of the Harden Quarries. In springtime the snowdrops appear in profusion about the ruins. From the Alnham to Alwinton road it is a strange sight to see the desolate Chapel and the old riggs, which tell of extensive medieval cultivation in the area. The old village has disappeared like that of neighbouring **Clennell,** the results of agricultural change and depopulation. On this same road above Alwinton and Clennell is a gaunt house called Wilkinson Park. It has no trees for shelter and dominates the entire landscape.

A lady left Clennell Hall in anger, and vowed that she would overlook her neighbours. By contrast Clennell Hall is close to the river Alwin and shrouded by trees. It is now a restaurant and country hotel with interesting surroundings. The monks of Newminster once had land at Kidland, and entered into an agreement with Thomas of Clennell about way-leave for their cattle and sheep. Clennells were there for centuries. William Clennell was constable of Harbottle Castle in 1434, and Percival Clennell led the men at the muster of 1538. He was the owner of Clennell tower in 1541 described as "newly reparelled and brattyshed. And also he ys in making of a new barmekyn about the same as his power will extend thereto."

The tower measures 30 feet by 22 feet, with a barrel vaulted basement and walls 6 feet thick. In 1568 a west wing added. This was 2 storeys high and the tower 3. An eastern wing was added also and later heightened. Plaster work of the sixteenth century, which depicts a hunting scene, still remains. Clennell Hall was very much altered from 1895, making it a much larger mansion built in characteristic stone; it has attractive gardens and woodland surroundings.

What were once routes for raiders and reivers provide pleasant walks for tourists and others. Now extensively wooded the landscape still shows Lynchets, riggs and other signs of ancient cultivation. Millstones were quarried from Harbottle Crags, mentioned in a survey of 1604.

HARBOTTLE CASTLE

Viewed from Harbottle Crags or from Clennell Street, Harbottle Castle seems lost in the immense space of the area. Yet it can be seen why the site was chosen for a fortress. It is situated on high ground and the river Coquet loops round it with the name of Devil's elbow.

There is a road following the Coquet from Dere Street (the main Roman road into Scotland), which joins Clennell Street at Alwinton with another road coming from the east linking the Borderland towers. So the Umfravilles moved from Elsdon to this place, which was originally a motte and bailey castle.

In 1157 Henry II ordered Odinel de Umfraville to build a castle here as part of his policy to replace timber constructions with stone. This may have taken a considerable time, and permission was granted from the Crown for further fortification in 1220.

The motte was on the south side of the eminence, overlooking the village. Here was a shell keep with a projecting entrance on the west. A substantial rampart and wall followed the perimeter to the north tower, and beneath was a very deep ditch. The axis for the defences was the 100 yards from the keep, and a strong wall was constructed from the north tower directly to the keep, which was surrounded by another deep ditch. The eastern half of the site was a barmkin, a defensive enclosure for cattle, under the observation and protection of the keep. The entrance to this was from a lower approach on the eastern side.

Then there was a gate and gate tower controlling access to the western half (the bailey) and yet another entrance on the west and within the walls to the keep or donjon.

The walls, ruinous today, were substantial, and it is necessary to walk the ramparts and climb the mounds to get any idea of the strength of the Castle. Within the walls were large and lofty buildings, now reduced to foundations. Harbottle resisted the Scots in 1296, but in 1319, after Bannockburn, it was captured by Robert Bruce. By agreement it was supposed to be dismantled, but this was not carried out. It was restored under Edward III and continued in use, but needed subsequent repairs.

In 1515 occurred an interesting event in the story of the Castle. Margaret Tudor, Queen of Scotland, was widowed in 1513 and later married the Earl of Angus (a Douglas). They were driven out in 1515, and took refuge at Harbottle, habitable but probably not very comfortable. On October 15th Margaret gave birth to a daughter, who was also called Margaret. She later married the Earl of Lennox, and became mother of Darnley, second husband of Mary Queen of Scots and father of James VI and I. He became King of England one hundred years after his great grandmother became Queen of Scotland wife of James IV.

In 1515 Queen Margaret was very ill after childbirth. Harbottle, at this time, had a garrison of eighty men. She was moved by litter to Cartington Castle and then to Morpeth, the Castle of Lord Dacre. It was difficult to keep castles in repair, and in 1543 it was reported —
"Harbottle Castle, being the key of Redesdale, is in such decay that the garrison cannot now lodge in it without great peril."

The Castle was taken into the hands of the Crown. In 1551 it is called the King's Majesty's Castle of Harbottle — Edward VI, who was engaged in Scottish Wars. The Castle had been partly repaired, but there was neither hall, nor kitchen, nor brewhouse, and the prison was insufficient. It was considered to be the best residence for the warden of the Middle Marches. Further surveys concluded it should be repaired, but Queen Elizabeth, though wishing to fortify the Borders, lacked the necessary finance.

In 1588 thieves broke into the Castle and carried away goods, and in 1596 it was so decayed that the captain had to move to Otterburn (still a military area). In 1604 when King James ruled both kingdoms it was "an old castle, much decayed", and he had no intention of restoring it. He granted all the Crown lands in Tynedale and Redesdale to a favourite, George Lord Home, who became the Earl of Dunbar.

The Castle was plundered for stone for houses and walls of the village, and the mansion which took the name of "Harbottle Castle".

Hodgson's sketch of 1830 shows stumps of masonry on castle mounds, looking strangely prehistoric, and some have fallen since that time.

ELSDON, in addition to the castle called Mote Hills, has another tower.
"The parsonage, which is called Elsdon Castle, is a strong old tower, which still externally retains much of its pristine form." Hodgson. It stands four storeys high on a hill to the west of the Elsdon Burn and the old Motte. It dominates the village, and in its time had a walled enclosure, now a sheltered garden. Shelter from the winds is much needed here.

On the south front of the tower, somewhat eroded is a shield with supporters and the lettering R D D R E D, which has been interpreted Robert Lord of Rede. The tower existed in the time of Sir Robert Umfraville who died in 1436. Hodgson thought it was the arms of Sir Robert Tailboys, since there was a shield similar to this at Whitton, and Tailboys also held

Black Middens Bastle

Elsdon Vicar's Pele

Elsdon Motte and Bailey Castle

Hepple Tower. I think that the arms were those of Umfraville, who were Wardens at times and held Harbottle Castle.

Hodgson says that the ground floor of Elsdon parsonage was a vaulted basement for cattle and horses; the kitchen and servants' quarters were on a stone flagged first floor, and above them the Rector's apartments and study.

In 1760 the Rector then resident was Dr. Dodgson, great grandfather of the author of "Alice in Wonderland". He gives us a graphic description of life there.

"Don't give yourself the trouble," he wrote, "to send my letters to this place, for 'tis almost impossible to receive 'em without sending 16 miles to fetch 'em. I am my own surgeon & apothecary; no creature of the profession within the same distance. A clog-maker combs my wig upon my curate's head for a block & his wife powders it with a dredging box. The vestibule of my castle is a low stable, above it a kitchen, in which are 2 beds. The curate and his wife lie in one, Margery the maid in the other. I lay in the parlour between two beds to keep me from being frozen to death. The village consists of my tower, an inn for Scottish carriers, five little farmhouses and a dozen more inhabited by poor people who receive the parish allowance, & superannuated shepherds. The principal farm houses are 5 or 6 miles apart. The whole country looks like a desert. The richest farmers are Scottish Dissenters and go to meeting house at Birdhope Crag, 10 miles from Elsdon. They do not interfere in ecclesiastical matters, nor study polemical divisions. They are hereditary Presbyterians, part of their estate rather than of enthusiasm. Those near Elsdon come to church, those near Birdhope to chapel, others of both sorts will go to the nearest church or conventicle. There is a good understanding & they will frequently do penance together in a white sheet, with a white wand, and barefoot in one of the coldest churches in England, and at the coldest season."

He goes on to say about the place —

"Not a tree or hedge within 12 miles to break the force of the wind. I have lost everything but my reason & cover my head with 3 nightcaps & a pair of stockings. As washing is cheap I wear 2 shirts, and for want of a wardrobe, hang my great coat on my back. There is to be a hopping on Thursday night — the conclusion of a pedlars' fair; a great concourse of braw lads and lasses who throw off their wooden shoes, shod with plates of iron and put on Scotch nichevers made of horse leather."

At this time the ballad makers were reviving memories of the Battle of Otterburn, fought near to Elsdon almost 600 years ago. Some of the dead were buried beneath Elsdon Church, which stands in the middle of the broad village green.

The parsonage tower still stands, now a private residence, at the north end of the village. On the south edge is the circular pound of stone, used for detaining stray cattle. In spite of Dr. Dodgson's strictures Elsdon is an attractive village, full of history. When the heather is in bloom on the hills, it is particularly delightful.

ELSDON CASTLE

Elsdon has the best example of a motte and bailey castle in the county, because it was not built upon after the early timber stage. It was constructed by Robert d'Umfraville as the chief place in Redesdale, which he held from the King in return for keeping the area free from robbers.

A most suitable place was chosen for the castle, the motte rising 90 feet above the Elsdon Burn, overlooking the burn and presumably a road. The Vicar's Pele, built some 300 years later, stands on high ground on the other (western) side of the burn, and bears the arms of Umfraville. Elsdon Castle was replaced by Harbottle Castle as the key defensive place, and so has been left as an impressive site for us to study. The size of the mound and the embankments of the bailey are remarkable after nine hundred years of wind and erosion.

The motte is some 50 feet across the top and the earthen rampart encloses about 900 square yards. It has been hollowed somewhat by later digging, but at the beginning of the castle it would have a strong timber palisade and within this the timber built hall of the Lord of Redesdale. Here would be living quarters and stores with a look-out tower. From this vantage point the countryside could be surveyed, and from the top of the mound the whole of the bailey or courtyard and the surrounding area could be covered by arrow fire.

The distance from the motte to the edge of the outer bailey was about 100 yards. If an extended bailey were needed, it was extended round the motte and not further away from it. Some castles, as at Alnwick, had a double bailey — one at each side of the motte.

The motte is surrounded by a ditch, which is deep and in parts wet, especially between the motte and the bailey, which is an enclosure of about half an acre and might be called "saddle shaped". The great curved ramparts rise to a height of thirty feet, and an outer ditch added to the defences. There was a deep ditch between it and the bailey, crossed by a hanging timber bridge which would have a guard house. The entrance to the bailey was probably between it and the motte.

In the bailey would be farm buildings, stores and further accommodation for people. The lord might not be able to rely on local men, and the castle dominated any village settlement. Outside the ditches on the counterscarp all round the castle would be further defences in the form of stakes, a palisade or even a hedge. So the castle would be strongly defended, and a photograph or diagram gives no idea of this. The defences have to be walked or climbed to get some idea of the difficulty of attack. The sheep and cattle, present day inhabitants, make winding paths round the motte, but a lower entry has been made on the southern side. The Umfravilles held Prudhoe Castle, also motte and bailey in origin.

Hodgson described Elsdon Castle —

"The Mote Hills are a very striking feature, both in the appearance and the history of this place: a deep & perennial verdure covers them."

He mentioned that local people had intruded on the place by digging for buried treasure. Among many things a blue and white fluted bowl was uncovered, many animal bones and Roman tablets. There is still a Roman memorial stone in Elsdon Church. In 1823 the Duke of Northumberland had purchased the site, improved the road and built a bridge over the burn. The villagers at one time practised archery in the castle area, and it is said, courts were held.

On my last wander round the site, the remains of snow brought out the contours of the land and the old plough riggs. I disturbed a big dog fox from his noon day snooze with the hounds far away. He languidly got up from almost beneath my feet and walked away. From the bailey he turned round and looked at me on the motte. The old defences were no problem to him, and the castle provided a good hiding place as well as a viewpoint.

The Elston Area has a collection of strong houses or bastles, some difficult to discover. One that can be reached, by a winding road south eastwards from the castle, is Whitlees. It stands on high ground with a walled enclosure, now in an area of forest. It is used as a barn and somewhat altered for the purpose. The walls are 4½ feet thick, built of random rubble with very large quoins or cornerstones, some of which are 4 feet in length. This is the usual style for this type of building. It had a timber upper floor carried on an offset from all four walls. The original doorway was at the eastern end, with probably a fireplace on the floor above. It is impressive in its primitive strength and its outlandish position.

To the north of Elsdon in the military area, with access forbidden when red flags are flying, are a number of peles and bastles. The road from Elsdon rises above the castle to a height from which the whole area can be viewed; then it falls to the walls of Billsmoor Deer Park, which belonged to Mr. Orde of Nunnykirk. The high walls encompass some seven miles of an area with trees and little valleys.

A road leads off westwards into the range near Dunn's Farm, once a region of mining and quarrying. The farm at Raw has a pele tower that is still used as a farm building, but has not been inhabited by human beings since an old lady, Margaret Crozier, was murdered there in 1791. The murderer, William Winter, was arrested and sentenced to death at Newcastle. His body was exhibited on a gibbet at Harwood Head, near the base of the Steng Cross. This is on the Morpeth road, and said to be within sight of the place of the crime, but binoculars are necessary. The distance is about five miles. From this same vantage point Rothley Castle, an eighteenth century folly, can also be plainly seen and there are extensive views. Winter's Gibbet is on the edge of the National Trust property, and had been recently restored. It consists of a tall upright with a crosspiece on which hangs a carved wooden head called 'a stob'.

The old doorway at Raw is now covered by a farm building. The jambs had a rebate and tunnels for the wooden draw-bar, which Winter forced open. The door was pivoted and the pivot hole is still visible. It led into a basement which was vaulted. Stone steps have been erected to a door on the upper floor, which had a fireplace. The only original window to the east had carvings upon it, including a human head. The building measures 42 feet by 25 feet externally, and the lower walls are 5 feet in thickness.

High Shaw bastle stands 500 yards west of the farm of that name, and north of Raw. It is exactly the same size, but only the barrel vaulted basement remains. Access to the upper floor was from the basement by ladder. Iron House, 300 yards to the west, is of the same size, and is one of a group of buildings that are ruined and deserted. At the first floor level is an offset for the floor and a projecting stone for the hearth.

Crag is an isolated farm one mile to the north on the miltary range road, which eventually leads to Holystone. One of the buildings of the farm is a ruined bastle with a complete vaulted basement, still used for farm purposes. Access to the upper floor was by a narrow stair in the thickness of the west wall, leading from the doorway. Within the military area are others that have been completely ruined before the survey was made. It is now an area for sheep, whose grazing is anything but peaceful. They seem to get used to gun fire and the shattering sounds of jet aircraft. There is a respite from gun fire at lambing time, but it soon begins again. The military range extends to Holystone and Harbottle, then to Alwinton and along the river Coquet to its source near Chew Green, where there are the remains of Roman military camps.

South of Harbottle on a forest clad hillside is Woodhouse Pele, standing roofless near Holystone Grange. It has a date stone with 1602 over the doorway, but this is not its original place and it may not be the original date. It was rebuilt at the beginning of this century and the spiral stair was altered. The walls were built of random rubble with squared quoins and the basement was barrel vaulted. The initials W P over the door stand for William Potte. The doorway has a double check and double bar holes. The door at the west end was inserted later approached by a ramp. The original upper door, probably on the south side, has gone. Two windows in the south wall had slots for iron bars. The building measures 40 feet by 25 feet, and the walls are 5 feet in thickness on the ground floor, but thinner above the first floor. It is tall enough to have had a loft storey like Hole.

On the opposite side of the Coquet from Woodhouse was the tower of Farnham, held in 1415 by Roger Horsley, and in 1541 stated to be in good repair, but it has gone, and the stone embodied in a farm house.

On the same side of the Coquet was another strong house at Sharperton. It was a ruined stone building with walls about 4½ feet thick, with external dimensions of 36 feet by 25 feet. It had been re-built in the seventeenth century, was again ruined and has now been embodied in a modern house.

Following the river Coquet leads to Harbottle, the most important of the Border strongholds in this area. Observed from a footpath by the river from Harbottle to Alwinton its strength and strategic position are obvious, but it is ruinous today.

BELLINGHAM is situated in hill country just north of the meeting of the rivers Rede and North Tyne. The river valleys provided routes into the area from Scotland, and for long periods of time the land belonged to the Scottish King.

Bellingham Castle was probably built by a family of that name in the early twelfth century. It was a motte and bailey type in a key position but it has disappeared. A mound on the Hareshaw burn opposite the station is supposed to be the site, but the railway and mining affected the area. These have gone also, and Bellingham now is mainly a market centre. It is also important to tourism on the route to Kielder Reservoir and Forest. The Pennine Way passes through and this attracts ramblers. There is a scatter of towers and bastles in the region.

The church has a stone vaulted roof, which is unusual but characteristic of this part of the county. It is a centre for the sale of cattle and sheep; a public house is called the ''Black Bull''.

In 1263 Sir Richard Bellingham held the manor and castle of Bellingham by service as forester in North Tynedale to the Kings of Scotland. The Bellingham shield carried three bugles or hunting horns and deer roamed the royal forest.

WARK ON TYNE

Another motte and bailey castle was established during the same period at Wark on Tyne, probably by Henry, Earl of Huntingdon. Tynedale was held as a fief by the King of Scotland from the King of England. So Scottish justices held courts at Wark Castle. It was raised on a flat topped natural hill south of the village and close to the North Tyne.

The motte was on the N.W. and the ditch between it and the bailey can still be detected, though the land has been much levelled to take the later farmhouse. Parts of the mounds of the bailey still rise from 25 to 40 feet above ground level and appear impressive from the old school. A stone tower was later erected on the mound — the early castle was timbered — and in 1415 the tower of Wark in Tynedale belonged to Sir Thomas Grey of Heton. An old mansion and fortress is mentioned in 1541, where the keeper of Tynedale appointed times for holding courts of justice.

HESLEYSIDE

Another tower on the North Tyne was at Hesleyside. In 1541 it was described as the only one still standing in the area. There was a garrison of 50 men there in 1525, when it was attacked by the Scots. It belonged to the Charlton family, and it had a mansion attached to it on the east side. The tower was demolished and the mansion embodied in the later country house, which had secret chambers and hide-holes.

Hesleyside suffered two fires in the eighteenth century, so there was much rebuilding and landscaping. The present house seems to have forgotten its turbulent past; one may get a reminder of it at Wallington Hall from one of Bell Scott's murals — the Charlton Spur. A Charlton squire among his sons at table, lifts the lid of a great dish expecting food and finds a spur. The hint was to get hunting or raiding to provide the meat for a meal.

TARSET CASTLE

On the other (east) side of the river and north of Bellingham is yet another derelict castle at Tarset. It overlooks the Tarset burn, and the site was altered by the development of the Border Counties Railway more than a century ago. This adds another ditch to the west of the castle mound.

In 1267/8 Henry III granted John Comyn, later a claimant to the Scottish crown, a licence to crenellate the hall he intended to build at Tarset. Very little has been recorded about it, but in 1523 it was held by Sir Ralph Fenwick with 80 men. He was driven out by William Charlton of Bellingham and his men, but in 1525 he came back with Tynedale men and some Scots. The castle was destroyed and its stone used for other buildings, till nothing was left but grass grown heaps. Excavations in 1888 located a secret tunnel or sewer, but the stone was taken away.

A plan of 1773 shows the hall to be a rectangular building with 4 corner towers, surrounded by an outer wall; a deep ditch circles the site from the steep bank of the burn to the railway cutting on the west side. The fortification overlooked a number of approach ways.

DALLY CASTLE belonged to the manor of Chirdon, and the Chirdon burn now flows by its ruins, at one time driving the water-mill. It is now a forestry area, but the ruins are close to the road and easy to see. In 1237 Hugh Bolbec complained to Henry III that Sir David Lindsay was building a strong house on the King of Scotland's land in Tynedale, and it was a threat to the English. It has been thought that this might be at Chirdon but there no evidence remains; whereas at Dally there is plenty.

The castle was built on a kaim or glacial ridge, cut off by a ditch on the western side; the stream cuts the eastern end. The original castle might be called a hall-house, measuring 70 feet from east to west, and 40 feet from north to south. The walls are about 6 feet in thickness, and there are remains of another building at the eastern end, 30 feet by 15 feet, which was either a barn or chapel. The walls of the main building contained fishtail loopholes that had been carefully blocked when the building was further developed.

At the N.W. end of the castle a turret about 20 feet square was added, and at the N.E. end another of similar size was added later in the fourteenth century. The north wall was buttressed and there are walls of uncertain date added to the south wall. Down the centre of the ground floor were a series of columns that supported the main beam. Ironically there were taken away to build a pigsty in the last century. The upper floor also had a colonnade, and there was presumably a rampart walk for defensive activity. It gives an impression of strength and solidity. It seems to have been occupied into the reign of James I, but later it fell into ruins. Stones from it were used to build the mill and other buildings.

The survey of 1541 mentions Bellingham as the town and "place of common resort for Tyndall", but does not mention a castle there; only that at Hesleyside was a little tower. Tarset and Wark castles had suffered. Tarset had been burnt and Wark was described as "as old mansion and appearance of a fortresse". The men of Tynedale inhabited strong timber houses in difficult places. However, it seems since that time stone houses or bastles have been built; or perhaps the surveyors did not look into the most dangerous areas.

A number of these still remain. The ones at Donkleywood and Camp Cottage are reduced almost to foundations, but there are two much better buildings at Gatehouse. The south bastle there was converted into a farmhouse in the last century, putting in larger windows and doors. The original door on the N.W. side has been blocked and a further building was added. The building is now roofless and the walls shaky, so that close investigation is dangerous.

The north bastle on higher ground is in much better condition with roof and first floor intact. The walls are built of random rubble, and the original ground floor doorway was in the N.E. end with tunnels for drawbars. The upper storey is approached by outside stone steps with small windows on either side of the door. One has a blind arch cut into the lintel and the other has holes for bars. The upper floor is carried on timber beams, rough hewn, which can be inspected from the light of a door at the west end. At this end also was the first floor fireplace. Now serving as a store, the ground floor was once used to house the cattle.

Black Middens is a mile N.W. of Gatehouse, standing on higher ground and reached by a forestry road. The bastle has been taken over by English Heritage and carefully restored, except the roof which is left open. This allows a much closer inspection of the structure since these buildings are normally gloomy inside when the roof is sound.
It has been described as a late sixteenth century farmhouse to protect a family in a lawless area, and there are other buildings to the south. The bastle measures 36 feet by 24 feet with thick walls, constructed of large stones. The original ground floor doorway in the east end is now blocked. It was narrow and strongly barred. The two doorways on the south side are later and now closed by metal grilles in the style of the "yett". A stone stairway leads to the original upper door, which has bar holes and the lintel seems to have been a re-used window head. There are two small windows on this same wall and floor, which was timber supported by offsets in the walls. The upper walls are narrower and can now be inspected from a platform. Within the walls are the ends of cruck timbers that supported the original roof. At the west end is corbelling that supported the fireplace. The east end has two cavities that were probably wall cupboards. From its setting and structure Black Middens is one of the best of such buildings for inspection. One mile N.W. is so called Corbie Castle, hidden in the Tarset Forest area. This is reduced to the ground floor level, but it is evident that it was vaulted. Its measurements are similar to those of Black Middens.

Simonburn Tower was situated on a ridge to the N.W. of the village, now approached by a narrow road, and the ruins stand deep in trees. The tower was substantial and protected by steep slopes and water. The N.E. face of the tower still stands fairly high for it was partly rebuilt in the eighteenth century as a folly or "eyecatcher" from neighbouring Nunwick Hall. The ruins are difficult to sort out, but the tower was some 35 feet in width and the ground floor had an internal barrel vault of 16 feet span. The N.W. wall was nearly 10 feet thick and contained the entrance with a mural guard chamber and spiral stair. In 1541 the report reads —
"At Symondburne ys a strong tour of force house (storey) high" belonging to Sir William Heron, "and it standeth of a very strong ground of myle from Chypchase upon the west syde of northe tyne & ys in measurable good repac'ons".
Hodgson wrote that the "castle" was sold by Herons to Allgoods, but it had partly been pulled down by local people in what he called insatiable greed for buried treasure and got nothing but rubbish for their pains. In 1766, he says, part of the west end was rebuilt with two small turrets at the angles.
In 1541 there was a parsonage tower in good repair at Simonburn and Sir William Heron had a bastle house at Hall Barns in good condition.

CHIPCHASE
The Herons also held Chipchase described as "a fare tower and a manor of stone warke joyned thereunto". Viewed southwards from Wark this Castle provides a very fine spectacle, since a Jacobean house was added to it with other extensions later. It has properly been described as a tower house and built in the fourteenth century.
Rectangular in shape it measures 51½ feet from north to south and 34 feet from east to west. It rises to a height of 50 feet to the parapet walk and the corner turrets rise a further 10 feet, so that it is a very imposing building and well constructed. The entrance, on the east side, was tall enough to admit a man on horseback. The heavy door was double barred and strengthened by a timber portcullis, which is still there. The vaulted basement is 34 feet long by 16 feet wide and 12½ feet high. The walls are nine feet in thickness and there is a trapdoor at the north end. There is a spiral staircase from the entrance which rises through three more floor levels to the battlements. On the first floor above the entrance is a guard room, from

which the portcullis could be controlled. It had the purpose of closing the entrance when the door was open, thus providing ventilation when animals were kept below. There is a well on the ground floor.

The first floor had a large room, lighted only by slits and was probably for storage. The lower hall was on the second floor and the upper hall on the third floor. At these upper levels were a number of apartments within the thickness of the walls. These were kitchen, chapel, private rooms and garderobe. The chapel is L shaped and a skew window enabled occupants to see what was happening at the altar. The upper and lower halls had fireplaces and larger windows, which could be shuttered. At roof level the battlements are machicolated, like the corner turrets, which project beyond the walls. Each turret had a guard room, and the rampart walk went round the whole of the roof. The building is very impressive and well preserved. Cuthbert Heron from 1621 built a manor house to the south east of the tower which has been described as "the finest example of the architecture of its time in Northumberland", and it was not in any way defensive. The Castle is occasionally open to the public in summer time.

Haughton Castle is situated on the west bank of the North Tyne, two miles from Chipchase and opposite Barrasford to which it was for long connected by a ferry. The bridge crossings of the river are few, but the view of Haughton from the other side of the river shows its splendid setting in the trees with the old paper mill below.

The castle was not of primary importance. In 1541 it is described —

"At Hawghton 2 miles S.E. from Simonburn standeth the walls of an olde castell or fortresse very strong, but the roofes & floores thereof bene decayed & gone. And an old barmkin p'tely decayed in the walls thereof", belonging to Sir John Widdrington. It had been raided in 1541 and suffered again in 1587. Later it was restored by Captain Smith.

Haughton, however, is unusual among English castles from its shape — great length and height, emphasized by its narrowness. The embattled turrets at each corner rise above the walls, but unusual is a series of five pointed arches on each side resting on buttresses, which screened the long machicolations. Defences were added to a hall-house in the mid thirteenth century, when relations between England and Scotland were very tense. It is unusual since hall houses, made of timber, have not survived, whereas later stone towers have. The tower house is the hall house set on end, so that height is the longest dimension.

At Haughton the arches were filled in and the walls were thickened and heightened. The turrets were carried above the roof, and a new turret was added in the middle of the south side, higher still.

The walls were provided with parapet walks and crenellations. This was the work of Gerald Widdrington from 1341, who was also fortifying his manor house at Widdrington.

Haughton measures 106 feet by 44 feet plus the turrets. With the infilling of the arches the basement walls are 10 feet thick. This floor is divided by a wall longways, and has two parallel ribbed vaults. A medieval cross wall continues upwards dividing the hall from the chambers. The basement was lit by loops and a cross loop in the S.W. corner guarded the entrance. The N.E. turret contains 7 small chambers one above the other. The S.W. turret contained the spiral stair to the various levels and the roof. The S.E. turret also contained chambers, including two oratories. The first floor contained the Hall with gallery and end chambers. The second floor became the principal floor when the castle was heightened. The Hall was at the west end with the great chamber and others at the east end. There were two levels on each main floor for the smaller chambers. Each turret had a chamber above roof level, which is about 60 feet high, and the top of the turrets 10 feet higher.

The barmkin has disappeared, but the height above the river gives some idea of the strength of the site. The village near the castle has disappeared, but the ruins of the chapel remain as a landscape feature.

Here, as at Cocklaw Tower, Roman stone from the Wall was used in the buildings.

COCKLAW

Cocklaw Tower, which can be seen from Chollerton Church, is a tower house of the style of Chipchase and Belsay, but not so impressive, since it is ruinous and the corner towers have disappeared. It now stands to a height of 40 feet and has deteriorated, since a century ago the vaulted basement was intact and painted plasterwork was recorded on the walls of

Cocklaw Tower

Chipchase Castle

Bellister Castle

upper apartments, one being called the "Painted Room". It looks forlorn, having suffered from the smoke of the railway and lime kilns, but the stonework is excellent.

The dimensions are $50\frac{1}{2}$ feet by $34\frac{1}{2}$ feet, and there is an offset outside the walls 10 feet from the ground. The entrance is on the south side with a pointed vault inside from which a door leads into the basement, measuring 31 feet by 21 feet with a single loop at the north end. On the left of the entrance porch was a vaulted chamber 8 feet by 5 feet, formerly entered from a trap in the first floor and called a dungeon, but perhaps a "safe". On the right a door led on to the spiral stair, giving access to upper floors and the roof. The first floor had the hall with fireplace and windows. On the east side was a doorway, which could be entered from outside by a ladder. The painted room was at the south end. The windows had bars and could be shuttered. There were similar arrangements on the second floor. The roof had a parapet walk and turrets, and there was machicolation over the entrance.

Cocklaw Tower was one of the possessions of the Errington family, who held Beaufront, Sandhoe and Errington. Armstrong's Map of 1769 gives Errington Hall the title of "Castle". There was a Beaufront Castle in 1415, but the present Beaufront Castle was built to the design of John Dobson in the last century.

At this stage we look at the Roman Wall — a series of forts, milecastles, turrets, walls and ditches that stretched across the entire country from mouth of Tyne to the Solway. It was known and written about, but not used except as a quarry for stones. Examples of this are at Carrawburgh near the Roman fort, where the farmhouse is partly built of Roman stone. Old features are evident in the structure.

In 1541 "At the Carrowe is a toure & stone house" which belonged to the King and formerly to Hexham Priory. It was in decay and so was the old tower at Sewingshields, which belonged to John Heron of Chipchase. The site of the castle can be picked out near the farm when viewed from the Roman Wall, where other medieval buildings have been found, constructed of Roman Stone. At Housesteads the south gate of the Roman fort was converted into a tower and used by raiders and horse thieves later. At Bradley, south of the Wall in 1541 "a stone house . . . of Nicholas Carrowe, lyeth waste & unplenished". However, at Settlingstones the tower of William Carnaby was in good repair.

THIRLWALL

At Walltown John Ridley's tower was in decay, but at **Thirlwall** the tower of Robert Thirlwall was well maintained. This still stands as a remarkable structure, which accounts for the complete disappearance of the Roman Wall in the immediate vicinity. The stone has all gone into the castle, which stands on high ground above the Tipalt Burn. It was acquired by the Swinburnes, and sold to the Earl of Carlisle.

Hodgson found it in ruinous condition — a lot of stone had been taken to build cottages and treasure seekers had done damage. The castle overlooked one of the main routes of the Scots and the river system was not much of a hindrance. In 1369 it appears as "the castrum de Thirlwall". The term "Thirlwall" was used for the Wall itself and the family at the Castle.

The basement was gloomy, only lighted by narrow slits. The internal measurements are 46 feet from north to south, and 19 feet from east to west, with walls 9 feet in thickness. A tower 14 feet by 15 feet juts out on the east side, covering the entrance at the N.E. angle, where there was a tower. The stair within the wall led to the first floor of the N.W. tower, beneath which was a dungeon. The ground floor appears not to have been vaulted, and there were two floors above. Decay in the interior makes it difficult to sort out. Part of the tower fell over the Tipalt in 1831, and there have since been other falls. The castle is in an interesting situation near the railway, and is an important feature on the Wall. It ought to be taken over by English Heritage, because it shows what happened to the Roman Wall.

Having reached the Cumbrian Border, the makers of the 1541 survey turned back along the South Tyne.

Blenkinsop Castle dates back to 1339 when "Thomas de Blencansopp" obtained a licence to crenellate his mansion "on the borders of Scotland". In 1415 it is mentioned among the list of Border Castles, belonging to John de Blenkinsope. In 1488 his son gave it into the custody of Henry Percy, Earl of Northumberland, who was Warden of the West and Middle

Featherstone Castle

Hole Bastle

Willimoteswick Castle

Marches. The west area included Cumbria, and Blenkinsop was a suitable place for a garrison. In 1541 it was reported as belonging to John Blenkinsop, decayed in the roof and not in good repair.

The Blenkinsops may well have left the place for the hall or Bellister Castle, and allowed it to decay. Wallis, about 1769, described it as on an eminence with a high wall and a deep ditch. It had a vaulted basement with external measurements 55 feet by 40 feet with an additional tower. The outer wall was something like 12 feet from the tower and stood to the same height, but on the west it has been taken down.

Hodgson reported that it was used to house labourers, until a new dwelling house in castellated style was added in the nineteenth century. Then it was used as the residence of the agent for the colliery. Blenkinsop is said to be haunted by the ghost of a lovely white lady, like Meg o' Meldon, seeking her lost treasure. The castle was built from Roman stone and was supposed to have a secret tunnel.

In 1541 the Blenkinsops had a bastle house at **Bellister,** which was kept in good repair. It stood on a motte and was defended by a deep ditch. The tower was built from Roman stone and was barrel vaulted in the basement. The walls were 7 feet thick. In the seventeenth century a mansion was added to it, and some of the old windows can be detected. Hodgson described it as "a grey and goodly pile of ruined towers, with modern inhabited additions in the castellated style and in good taste".

It has been rebuilt in modern times after severe damage by fire. Situated among trees and gardens it now has an attractive setting. Here too is the legend of the ghost of a "Grey man". He was a wandering minstrel who came to the castle; when he left the lord of the castle, suspicious of him as a possible spy, sent sleuth hounds after him and he was savaged to death, before his pursuers could catch up. Local people claimed to have heard the baying of dogs and the cries of the man. They also supposed another secret tunnel, probably a drain.

In 1541 at **Featherstonehaugh** was a tower belonging to Alexander Featherstonehaugh, which was kept in good repair. The family were often involved in border raids and local feuds, including an affray with the Ridleys.

There was a hall house at Featherstonehaugh and in the fourteenth century Thomas of Featherstonehaugh built a tower, which was L shaped with a vaulted basement. Three more towers were added to it in later times with offices, apartments and other buildings in castellated style. The new owner, James Wallace, had these built. Hodgson has a fine engraving of the Castle in his history of the area. The old tower was the central part and other buildings conformed in style. A castellated wall surrounded the lawns and gardens. The setting is now beautiful parkland, close to the waters of South Tyne. It is interesting that these three castles, close together, keep the castle style of architecture. Featherstone too is ghosted by a murdered bridal party.

Haltwhistle stands on high ground above the South Tyne. It was a barony in medieval times, and Castle Hill is the site of the early motte, which did not develop into a grand stone castle, since the families of De Roos and Musgrave had greater estates elsewhere.

The mound is a striking feature of the place with its steep sides, partly man made. An earthern rampart ran round the top, which measures roughly 200 feet E.W. and 75 feet N.S. It is very similar to neighbouring Bellister and more distant Elsdon. In 1541 "At Hawtewysle is a tour of the Inheritance of Sir William Musgrave knighte in measurable good rep'ac'ons."; and it was there in 1416. Tomlinson, in 1888, described it as a plain stone building "with a loop holed turret built on corbels". The old roof consisted of flagstones on heavy oaken beams and fixed with sheep shank bones. The floors were made of flags laid across roughly hewn beams. A spiral stair led to the upper part of the tower. This has been demolished.

Hodgson wrote that there were two tower houses in the main street of Haltwhistle and both were inns. The present Red Lion Hotel is the surviving example. Another to the east has been demolished.

East of Haltwhistle and south of the Tyne, evident from both road and railway is **Willimoteswick,** where Bishop Nicholas Ridley was born.

In 1541 "at Willymonnteswyke ys a good tower and a stone house ioynyne thereunto of the inheritance of Nycolas Rydley kepte in good rep'ac'ons".

It is a particularly interesting example because the gatehouse still stands, the barmkin is now the farmyard and the present old farm house has turrets at either end. It was not among the Castles and Towers of the 1415 list.

The courtyard measures some 56 feet by 33 feet, and is entered by the gatehouse at the N.E. corner, which measures 40 feet by 22 feet. There is a carriage entrance 10 feet wide with barholes for a stout bar to the doors. Within are two doorways on the north side, one leading to a guardroom and the other to spiral stairs. These rise to 3 floors and the roof. The battlements project on corbelling and some of the water-spouts are made to look like guns. The manor house within has suffered much alteration, but the end towers stand up in a strange fashion. They measure 17 feet by 8 feet with a slight batter. The stonework of the quoins is excellent, and they stand 40 feet high. At one time they had battlements and stairs within. One had a gardrobe.

Extra buildings have been added to the manor house. An inventory of 1585 lists the rooms as Inner Chamber, Great Chamber, Vault Chamber, Chamber above the stairhead, other chambers for servants, Parlour, Buttery, Kitchen and Hall. Books were the Bible and Foxe's Book of Martyrs, which records the burning of Bishop Ridley in 1555.

Unthank Hall also belonged to the Ridleys, but there is no trace of the old tower remaining.

LANGLEY

Next in order on the 1541 survey was Langley Castle, which belonged to King Henry VIII, acquired from Thomas, Earl of Northumberland.

"All the roofs and floors thereof be decayed wasted & gone and nothing remains, but only the walls: and it stands in a very convenient place for the defence of the incourses of the Scots of Liddisdale and of the thieves of Tindale, Gilsland and Bewcastle, when they ride to steal or spoil within the Bishopric of Duresme".

In 1550 George Heron, keeper of Tynedale, used his own castle. It was recommended that the King's own castle should be put in order for any other person in the same capacity. But it seems little was done, and in 1608 it was reported that "the walls stand firm and fast; but the covering and the outward work are utterly ruined, and so have been time out of mind."

It was acquired by the Percies by marriage to the Lucy family, and damaged in the Rebellion of 1405. The interior was burnt and Hodgson observed the reddened stonework. He greatly admired the structure and the situation.

The central building was a hall house measuring 82 feet by 25 feet internally with walls 7 feet thick. At each corner was a tower 21 feet square, jutting out on the east and west sides, but not extending beyond the north and south ends or sides, where there were buttresses at the junctures. There was a stair tower on the east front, with a portcullis to reinforce the doors. The vaulted basement housed the kitchens and stores. The ground floors of the towers were also vaulted. Within the central area above the kitchen were 3 floors whereas in the towers, with small rooms, there were 4 floors above the vaulted basement. The towers stood 66 feet high, and the s.w. tower contained a series of garderobes, said to be one of the finest collections of any castle.

Hodgson became rather lyrical about Langley Castle —

"While I gaze on it, even at a great distance, seems to bid a stern defiance to the attacks of time, as if determined once again to resume its roof and hang out over its battlements its blue flag and pillared canopy of morning smoke, as emblems that joy and high minded hospitality have returned to reside in it."

Strangely enouth some 50 years after he wrote, it was expensively and lovingly restored by Cadwallader John Bates, author of the Border Holds of Northumberland. Today, a century later, it still offers hospitality as a hotel and restaurant. It is in an attractive woodland setting and is described as "the only medieval fortified Castle Hotel in England." Lumley Castle might demur!

On the River Allen, south of both Willimoteswick and Langley is **Staward "Pele".** In the sixteenth century reports of Border Defences it is suggested how cheaply a tower could be restored.

In 1326 Edward II brought Staward and employed Thomas Featherstonehaugh, keeper of North Tynedale to restore it with a curtain wall and gate house of three floors. £100 was to be paid and timber provided, but Thomas was soon asking for more because of difficulties of transport and labour.

It was high over the river on a jutting promontory, cut off by a ditch and the gateway defended by drawbridge and portcullis. Now it is a ruin but the scenery is beautiful.

At **Newborough** in 1541 was a tower of Lord Burrow, which was in good repair. There are the remains of a tower 42 feet by 33 feet among the buildings of Thornton Farm, at Newborough.

The 1541 survey mentions "Mykle Swinburne", which had a great tower belonging to Sir John Widdrington, "but all the rooffes & floores thereof bene decayed & nothing standinge but the walles."

It was recorded in 1415 as a fortalice. Roger de Widdrington had obtained a licence to crenellate his mansion at West Swinburne in 1346 and it was surrounded by a strong wall. Widdringtons continued to live there and in 1596 Sir Robert Kerr of Cessford broke into Swinburne Castle and

"sounding his trumpet upon the top of the house, when he had taken his pleasure, went his way," rescuing James Young, alias James of the Coave, who was a prisoner there. There was bad blood between the Kerrs and the Widdringtons. The tower on the edge of the Swin Burn was pulled down to make way for a later hall, which in turn has been demolished.

At Little Swinburne in 1541 was "a lytle tower" belonging to Thomas Middleton of Belsay, "decayed in the roofes". It was not listed in 1415, but was built soon after and very similar to the towers of Hepple and Tosson. It has been very much robbed, but the ruins are still sufficient to give some idea of the style and dimensions — 40 feet from north to south and 27 feet from east to west, with walls 7 feet thick. The doorway was at the N.E. corner, opening into a passage with one door leading to the stair and the other to the vaulted basement. Fireplaces show that there were 2 other floor levels above. There were other buildings and an enclosure. To the south is the site of a medieval fish pond. It attracted the attention of Edward Swinburne, who provided a drawing of it to illustrate Hodgson's History of Northumberland — an example of a romantic ruin.

The survey of 1541 mentions "Carre Cottes (Carrycoats) in the said Fylton Moor is another bastel house (of the King) in good repair." Filton and Tolland (Tone) were granted by Odinel de Umfraville to Newminister Abbey and in his charter "Derestrete runs between Filton and Tolland as far as Waterfall".

Dere Street was the Roman road that passes east of Great Swinburne and on to Fourlaws and Risingham. In medieval times it was both a road and a boundary. The lands of Newminster were confiscated by Henry VIII.

"At Fyton more is a bastel house called the Whitehouse" belonging to the King. There is a farmhouse of the same name today, and Waterfalls Farm is where the rebels of 1715 assembled.

The survey moves to Ritton, where there was a store house and a little barmekyn, once the property of Newminster monks and then the King. So was Greenleighton where there was another little stone house with a barmkin. Here an old chapel remains and mounds of earth, but Ritton Whitehouse Farm embodies the remains of the old tower. Rothley, not far away, also had a little tower of Henry VIII, but this was demolished in the eighteenth century by Sir Walter Blackett, when the present "folly" Rothley Castle was built.

At Hartington in 1541 there was "a stronge bastell house", belonging to Sir John Fenwick, which was in good repair. It still is, overlooking the Hart Burn, with modern windows and a roof that has been raised. The farm buildings have been converted into a garden centre and the old name "Harterton" is used for it.

Sir John Fenwick had another "lytle pele house or bastell" which was in good repair at a place called "Sawnes". The present name is "Fawns", and a farmhouse overlooks the site, which is quite remarkable.

At the north end is a motte, surrounded by a ditch, on which the tower was built; and to the south is a large bailey or barmkin, surrounded by a deep ditch and earthen bank. There are also the hollows of fish ponds. Other sites were no doubt moated, but this has been so well preserved as to be called unique.

At Wallington, in 1541, across the fields was

"a strong tower ad a stone house" belonging to Sir John Fenwick, which was in good repair. The remains of this are embodied in the cellars of Wallington Hall. Across the Wansbeck, in 1541, Thomas Fenwick owned a tower at Little Harle and it still stands as the oldest part of Little Harle Tower, a much enlarged mansion.

Capheaton Castle was mentioned in 1415, but not in 1541.

Leland called it "a faire castle" and another writer said "it was moated about, and had a drawbridge and was a place of resort in the moss trooping times, when the gentlemen of the country met together to oppose those felonious aggressors upon the goods and chattels of the country, having a beacon on its top to alarm the neighbourhood."

In 1668 it was used by Robert Trollop as a quarry in the construction of Capheaton Hall for Sir John Swinburne. So though the stone may be there it has taken a different form and there is nothing military about it. The ha-ha or sunken wall takes the place of the moat, and the chapel was allowed to remain as a ruin to embellish the landscape.

The Devil's Causeway passes to the east of Capheaton towards Shaftoe. At the east end of Shaftoe Hall is a medieval barrel vaulted stone tower. The vault is ribbed and strongly built with 2 storeys above. The ruins of the old village and chapel are to the west of the Hall.

Kirkwhelpington, on the Wansbeck, was described by John Hodgson, vicar and historian, as a neat village with a green and at the head of it the church with its buttressed tower and beyond "the little tower, the mansion of the vicarage", recorded in 1541.

The internal dimensions were 27 feet by 15 feet, but external would be 37 feet by 25 feet. It has an internal stair to the upper rooms. The building was altered and added to by different vicars. In 1771 Nathaniel Ellison converted part of the old tower into a kitchen. This still stands on the north of the building, now in private occupation.

In the churchyard on May 14 1826, was buried John Codling, parish clerk for 63 years, but he could be called a "castle" builder. Employed as a mason he worked in the building of Kielder Castle, a hunting or shooting lodge for the Duke of Northumberland. For Sir Walter Blackett of Wallington he was employed in the construction of Codger's Fort and Rothley Castle, both follies.

Hodgson also wrote that the only peel house at Kirkwhelpington was called Bolt House. It consisted of a byer or cow house below and the family apartments above. These were an upper room with a timber floor and a garret above, "both approached by stone stairs on the outside and the whole covered with thatch."

The doorway to the byer was under the stairs, indicating a later addition. The door was fastened by a strong bolt or bar, and there was a trap hole to the upper floor from below. "This", he adds, "was the character of the principal farm houses in Northumberland a hundred years since" i.e. 1700. This type of building would be called a "bastle" in the modern survey. Hodgson considered that these would be for lesser men and the "peels of the lairds" had stone vaulted basements and stone roofs.

He also described the now deserted village of West Whelpington, which "stood proudly on the northern margin of the Wansbeck . . . . It was of an oblong form, about 440 yards long & consisted of two rows of houses inclosing a large town green, near the centre of which a small circle probably points out the site of its cockpit, near which has stood a peel house about 23½ feet by 21½ feet on the inside, having very thick walls and a sort of yard or barmekin in front, apparently the only little fortified habitation which the place could ever boast of."

A man called Stote took over in the eighteenth century and "put out 15 farmers". In recent times, in face of quarrying, the village site has been partly excavated. But the quarry too has been abandoned, and the police now use it for small arms practice. Their "sleuth dogs" or Alsatians can also be seen in training over the Wanneys.

Still further westwards at Sweethope was another tower, which has disappeared. In 1541 here was a bastle house belonging to Sir John Fenwick, kept in good repair. There was another quite near at Hawick.

Hodgson wrote that Ray was in almost the same condition as West Whelpington "for it now consists of one principal house, in a very ruinous state, occupied by one family, a peel house, unoccupied, and traces of numerous dwellings." Later in the century Sir Charles Parsons came to Ray and built a new mansion. The railway to Bellingham was developed, but this has been closed and Parsons' house has been demolished. The walls of the old pele, measuring 30 feet by 25 feet, are still there, and I saw them inhabited by pheasants.

On the other side of the railway near here are what were medieval fish ponds. The area is rather empty of people — mainly grouse moors and forestry, but Lord Davenport has developed a perfumery, making use of the heather.

On the same estate at **Ottercops** are two bastle houses that have joined, making a building 55 feet long by 25 feet wide. Both parts of the building have external stairs of stone, and there has been considerable rebuilding. They are used for farm purposes. Ottercops, at a height of 1050 feet, is a suitable place to take a wide view of Border country. Roads from Newcastle, Corbridge and Bellingham converge on Otterburn. There were drove roads also. It was in this area nearly 600 years ago that the famous battle between Hotspur and Douglas was fought by moonlight, to become the subject for ballad and story. This was a military area in Roman times, where they encamped, trained and built roads. It is a modern military range with red flags flying. There is rifle and machine gun fire and the explosions of great guns. Jet fighters come screaming in so fast that their sound follows them, and the sheep have grown used to it.

However, lesser feuds are remembered such as the death of Percy Reed of Troughend, betrayed by the Halls and killed by the Croziers. Troughend tower was there in 1415, held by Will Buticom, but it has since been demolished.

Otterburn Tower was held by Sir Robert Umfraville, but it was replaced by a mansion of the Halls, now a hotel. It is an area of bastles and two remain at Rochester within the Roman fort. There are several at Evistones, a deserted village, and another at Rattenraw, a farmhouse. A bastle at Evistones was barrel vaulted and measured 40 feet by 24 feet with thick walls.

Above the River Rede N.W. of Otterburn and near Dere Street stands the gaunt ruins of Shittleheugh, which Hodgson called "the mansion house of the Reeds". The gables stand to full height, and the walls are of large coursed squared stones. The door on the south probably had a porch or stair. The ground floor had vent slits only, and at the west end had corbelling for a hearth on the first floor. There were other buildings and an enclosure. Shittleheugh is considered to be of higher quality than the normal bastle. It measures 44 feet by 22 feet.

Having traversed the outer areas and hill country, considered in the Survey of 1541, we have to look at the castles and towers not included, as not so much in danger and not in the defensive girdle.

ALNWICK

We turn to **ALNWICK** and Warkworth, castles of the Percies, which were much involved in Border Wars through the ages. **ALNWICK** was the site of the death of Malcolm Canmore, King of Scotland, in 1093. He was killed by Sheriff Morell in battle. Saint Leonard's Chapel marked the spot and later a cross was erected.

The northern approach to Alnwick provides the fine spectacle of the Castle, south of the River Aln and situated in parkland. In the eighteenth century it was very different — a steep descent to the river and rough land on the other side, steeply sloping. It was landscaped by Capability Brown, and the river was dammed at intervals to maintain a level of water in which the Castle could be reflected. The north curtain wall was lowered to allow a view of and from the Castle, to which the Earl (later Duke) of Northumberland had returned.

The castle area itself has not altered since the earliest castle — a motte and bailey was built by Ivo of Vesci about 1100 A.D. and strengthened by his grandson, William.

The motte was central, dividing the bailey into an east and west ward. About 1150 it was enclosed by a stone wall and a shell keep on the mound, replacing the timber structures. Parts of the old stonework can still be seen. This castle was besieged by William the Lion of Scotland in 1174, and here he was captured. The event is recorded on a stone by the way leading to Hulne Park.

In 1309-10 Henry Percy purchased Alnwick, and his son acquired Warkworth through marriage. The Percies had lands in Sussex and Yorkshire, now moving into Northumberland, where they were to grow mightily in the fourteenth century. They were experts in war and military fortification. By 1350 great changes had taken place at Alnwick. Henry Percy had added to the shell keep a cluster of seven towers, semi-circular in shape. One of these was attached to the new hall, built on the east side of the enclosure. Interval towers were added to stronger curtain walls and a middle gateway between the outer and inner wards. Henry, first Baron Percy, died in 1315, a year after Bannockburn in which he took part.

Northumberland was now open to continuous attacks from the Scots, and it was all the more necessary for his son, the second baron, to continue improving the fortifications. He strengthened the gatehouse of the heavily fortified keep by adding two polygonal towers, thus increasing the length of the entrance passage beyond the ditch and drawbridge. His other work was on the main entrance from the west into the outer ward. Here was a new gatehouse with polygonal towers fronted by a barbican with double towers. The barbican covers the ditch with entrance by drawbridge, and there were doors at each end of the structure. There were stone figures of warriors as defenders on the battlements. They were probably for ornamentation rather than deception of the enemy. The present figures are modern, replacing the medieval ones.

Pevsner considers the barbican to be the best in the country, and it deserves special attention from the visitor, who does not now enter this way. The drawbridge filled the entrance when raised and part went down into the ditch. There was a portcullis and guardrooms on either side of the entrance.

The Abbot's Tower is at the N.W. corner of the outer ward, used by the Abbot of Alnwick when he chose, now containing a military museum.

The Postern Tower, another fourteenth century tower, is eastwards of the keep, overlooking the moat and also houses a museum of antiquities. The Constable's Tower is at the eastern limit of the inner ward, and a turret on it is called 'Hotspur's Seat'. From the Postern Tower the wall stands to full height with a rampart walk.

The Castle suffered decay after the defeat of the first Earl and further still during the Wars of the Roses. The Percies preferred Warkworth in Northumberland, but were often in trouble.

The Wizard Earl, whose resources were used to finance Gunpowder Plot in 1605, spent a long time in the Tower of London. Sir Hugh Smithson, who became first Duke of Northumberland (1750-86), decided to use the Castle as a residence, and it was rebuilt in Gothic style. This is shown by the Canaletto painting now in the Castle. The fourth Duke (1847-65) disliked the style, and had the castle rebuilt to the designs of Anthony Salvin. His external work was considered to be more authentically medieval, but the interior was decorated with Victorian extravagance.

The Castle is open to the public in summer months and the apartments contain priceless treasures. Also for the price of a ticket the visitor is entitled to visit the parklands. These contain the ruins of Alnwick Abbey — only the gatehouse remains; and Hulne Priory, which can be seen from the walk to Brislee Tower or visited from the northern park gate. This was a Carmelite establishment dating from the thirteenth century. The walled enclosure still stands with a medieval tower dating from 1488 — the Prior's tower. There are the ruins of buildings and the chapel. The first Duke converted it into a garden centre with a summer house.

Alnwick itself has a medieval plan and it is a partially walled town. Hotspur's Tower, which was built after his time in the fifteenth century, is the genuine medieval gateway, whereas Pottergate has been rebuilt. The circuit of the walls can be traced with help from the Information Centre. The Bailiffgate was originally an outer enclosure of the Castle and the Church of Saint Michael stands at the west end. This is one of the best medieval churches in Northumberland, and has special connections with the Castle, which has its own chapel. Since so much time and money was spent on building and repairing fortifications, Northumberland is not renowned for the splendour of its churches.

At Shilbottle, south of Alnwick, west of the Church, are the remains of a vicar's Pele, embodied in a later vicarage. It was barrel vaulted with thick walls.

Attracting attention from the sea is Coquet Island with its lighthouse and white-washed buildings. The lighthouse has a medieval tower for its base and adjacent to it is a long medieval building, partly converted into cottages. The western part of the range had a vaulted basement 45 feet long and 14 feet wide internally with walls 3 feet thick. There was a stair to the upper floor. The eastern part of the range, about 50 feet in length, may have included a chapel with a priest's room. In 1415 the tower is recorded as belonging to the Prior of Tynemouth.

WARKWORTH CASTLE

"Warkworth is the epitome of the history of the castle, from its Norman origin to its practical identification in the later Middle Ages with the large manor house." (Hamilton Thompson).

The site of the Castle is a natural eminence around which the River Coquet loops in such a way that only the south front has no natural water defence. The Castle could be supplied easily by sea and the river bridge to the north of what was a medieval town was guarded by a bridge tower. The only easy access was from the south, and the Castle dominates the town.

There are steep slopes on three sides, accentuated by a moat except on the west where the slope was very steep. A deep moat was cut on the south side where was the main entrance.

The original castle of the twelfth century was of the motte and bailey type and, as at Alnwick through the ages, the original dimensions have been kept. The motte was at the north end, and the axe shaped bailey was to the south. Originally the fortifications were earth and timber, being replaced by stone later in the century.

In 1173 the Castle was captured by the Scots when the change was not complete, and it was too weak to resist attack. "They come to Warkworth, nor deign to stay there
For the castle was weak, the wall and the trench,
And Roger, the son of Richard, a valiant knight,
Had it in charge; but he could not defend it." (Fantosme).

In the thirteenth century the walling of the bailey was completed on a grand scale with high walls and flanking towers. There was also a strong battlemented gatehouse on the south side. On the motte the shell keep seems to have been neglected or it had suffered from subsidence. A new set of buildings appeared on the west side of the bailey — a great hall with solar and chapel to the south; and the kitchen, buttery, pantry and larder to the north. There were other service buildings, stores and stables across the courtyard.

When the Castle came into the hands of the Percies in 1332, it immediately assumed much greater importance since they had the task of defending the Marches and were engaged in ceaseless Wars against the Scots. A large garrison had to be provided for — both food and accommodation within the walls. One method was for the lord to build himself a great gatehouse as at Dunstanburgh, to control the fortress. The other method was to return to the motte, which the Percies did.

The tower house that was constructed was a manifestation of their wealth and power, symbolized by the Lion "Rampant", that looked down on the town and the sculpture that adorned the porch of the great hall.

"The essential quality required of the Percy keep was that it should include within the same building the whole range of domestic accommodation expected of a nobleman's household."

The Percy for whom the work was done was the first Earl of Northumberland, father of Harry Hotspur. There is nothing quite like it in this country. It has been described as ingenuous and extraordinary, shaped like a Maltese cross. The central shape is a square building with the corners cut. On each side at the centre has been added a small wing or extension, also with the corners cut away. These serve as both extensions and buttresses, suiting the shape of the round motte. The construction is an illustration of architecture of the highest quality which is better seen from without rather than within, by walking round outside the walls.

The keep has three storeys, providing very comfortable quarters for a great noble and his household. On the ground floor are extensive vaulted stores, cellars and a kitchen. On the first floor, which is much lighter, are another kitchen, the hall and chapel, which rise through two storeys. The great chamber, however, has the parlour above it. These rooms are arranged around a central vent, which like a skylight allows light to penetrate from the top downwards. Water is collected from roof drainage in stone tanks in the basement for flushing the sewers and swilling the floors. There were wells inside for water use in cooking, baking and washing. A slender tower rises some 30 feet above the roof and this could be used for observation. From a distance it appears like the top of a chimney, but the whole of the Castle combines artistically together.

Warkworth Castle is in its way a masterpiece. While the lower walls are of great strength and solidity, the upper floors are lighted by traceried windows. The long windows of the hall and chapel have no military look about them. Unfortunately the builders were not able to enjoy it for long, being involved in rebellion; and the projected collegiate chapel which divided the inner from the outer bailey, only rose a few feet above the foundations. This no doubt would have been another impressive building on the site, perhaps dividing different worlds and providing for the Percies in the next world — 'Esperance en Dieu' carved round the lion's neck was their motto. (Hope in God.)

After defeating the Scots at Humbleton, near Wooler, the Percies were in dispute with Henry IV about the ransoming of captives. (1402). In the following year Hotspur engaged in rebellion and was killed in battle at Shrewsbury July 21 1403. The Earl of Northumberland was pardoned, but engaged in conspiracy in 1405. The King arrived with a large army and newly invented cannon. These caused so much destruction that the Castle surrendered after the seventh discharge. The Earl had escaped to Scotland, but the King took over his castles — Alnwick, Warkworth, Prudhoe and Langley.

In 1416 Henry V restored Hotspur's son to the Earldom and property. Warkworth Castle was his favourite residence, and he was made Warden of the East March. Warkworth was involved with the Wars of the Roses, and in 1462 the Earl of Warwick used it as a base from which to attack other castles. For some years the Percies lost their lands and castles, but they were recovered.

In 1537 the Earl gave his estates to Henry VIII. We have a report which showed the Castle in good repair with a pair of iron gates at the entrance and a single gate at the postern. Some little repairs were necessary to the walls. Brewhouse and bakehouse were covered with "sclatts" and not lead. These were also the covering for the two large stables which had garners above them.

"Ther is a marvellous proper dongeon of 8 towers: all joyned in on a house togethers & well coveryd with leyd."

A horse mill was set up in the castle and prisoners were kept in the pit.

In 1543 Lord Parr, father of Henry VIII's sixth wife, stayed at Warkworth, which was much healthier than Alnwick. It seems that he resided in the buildings in the bailey and not in the keep.

In 1557 Queen Mary restored Thomas Percy, the sixth Earl, and he lived partly at Warkworth. The Castle was kept in reasonable repair, but the great hall and other buildings in the bailey were not. In 1569 the Earl joined the Northern Rebellion and had to take refuge in Scotland.

Warkworth was taken over by the Crown and although the keep was "well buylded of stone and covered with lead", the other buildings continued to decay. Sir John Forster, Warden of the Middle Marches, plundered the Castle for his own use.

The 7th Earl was put to death in 1572, the 8th was imprisoned in the Tower and so was the 9th after Gunpowder Plot. This Earl Henry had to raise money for a £30,000 fine to James I; and Warkworth was let to Sir Ralph Grey of Chillingham for 21 years. He did not live there and the bailey and its buildings were used as a farmyard. In 1617 James I and some lords who paid a visit to the Castle were sorry to see it in such a state. The King looked at the Percy lion and said, "This lyone houldes up this castle".

William Shakespeare had no doubt heard of the condition of Warkworth Castle, and in Henry IV, his play involving the siege of Warkworth 200 years before, it is described as "this worm-eaten hold of ragged stone". In fact, before the siege and the attention of the cannon, it must have been one of the finest buildings in the country.

In the Civil War the Castle was used and abused. Afterwards in 1672 it became a quarry, and 272 wagon loads of lead, timber and other materials were carried to Chirton to build a manor house. In the middle of the nineteenth century, however, Algernon the 4th Duke, who rebuilt Alnwick Castle, repaired the keep at Warkworth, and in 1922 it was placed in the care of the Ministry of Works. Today it is under the care of English Heritage, and it is glorious to see when the mound under the keep is aglow with daffodils. Sometimes the old pageantry appears with the Warkworth Summer Carnival. The H.M.S.O. booklet provides a valuable guide to the site. The visitor can pick out the various loopholes and arrow slits, the different type of towers about the perimeter wall and the different buildings within.

I wonder whether the keep of Warklworth Castle can have been used as a sundial. It is orientated North to South and East to West with a tower extension at each point of the compass. At Hesket Newmarket in Cumbria, Sir Wilfrid Lawson built a mansion of similar design for the purpose of telling the time. The shadows cast by the angles could determine the time in the days when there was no summertime alteration of the hours.

Warkworth provides for the pleasures of boating and half a mile upstream from the Castle is the Warkworth Hermitage, a dwelling and chapel cut out of the living rock in medieval times. It is well worth a visit; and so is Warkworth Church dating from Norman times. Its monuments include the effigy of a medieval knight within the church, and a huntsman of James I in the churchyard. The medieval bridge and bridge tower, reached by a short river walk, add to the antiquarian attractions of the town. The Castle provides a beautiful picture from the bridge or from the river in either direction — upstream to the

Warkworth Castle

Edlingham Castle – Interior

Haughton Castle

Hermitage or downstream to the port of Warkworth, which is Amble. It has provided a subject for many a painter and photographer.

Moving across country from Warkworth and Alnwick, the next place in line of defence in 1415 was **Lemmington Tower,** held by William of Beadnell. The hall is now visible from the Alnwick to Rothbury road and the old tower, still in good repair, is situated at the east end of the mansion. It has been converted into a chapel for a Catholic establishment — the Convent of the Sacred Heart. From the high road it looks in a low position but from the north the site looks quite different and defensive. Surprisingly the tower is bigger than Cocklaw or Chipchase, being 53 feet from east to west and 35 feet from north to south. At the east end it is 13 feet wider with a turret to provide an entrance and spiral stair. This contains 3 storeys as did the tower itself, 2 above the vaulted basement. This measures 43 feet long by 17 feet wide, lighted by a loop at the west end. The entrance is on the south, one door leading to the basement, another on the left to the spiral stair and one on the right to a guard room. This had a room above with a gardrobe. The upper storey has been altered and reroofed. No doubt the tower had turrets and battlements as at Cocklaw or Chipchase. Extra windows were inserted in the eighteenth century, when the mansion of the Fenwicks was built.

A mile and a half along the Alemouth road brings the Castle of Edlingham into view, situated between a railway viaduct and a medieval church.

EDLINGHAM CASTLE

The importance of this Castle has only recently been recognised.
In the Country History we read —
"The castle, although of diminutive dimensions, exhibits some of the arrangements of a defensive military structure as may be seen by the general plan. It comprises a rectangular courtyard with projections to the east and west, that to the east being the keep or tower with flanking walls connecting it with the north and south curtains. So placed the tower, as was frequently the case, occupied a position on the exterior of the site, commanding the country and imparting strength at the point likely to be assailed."

When I examined the site for a book on castles (1969), I wrote that the plan was wrong and that there was probably a hall house immediately north of the tower. The area was completely overgrown with great ash trees, thorns, bushes and nettles, but one tall rib of the building stood up high. Another factor was that an inventory of 1572 detailed a number of rooms that obviously could not be fitted into the tower — the hall, the buttery, the parlour, the broad chamber, the wainscot chamber, the painted chamber, the kitchen, the brewhouse, the bake house. The inventory was connected with the will of Thomas Swinburne, who lived there and wished to be buried in the church. The apartments seem to refer to a hall house and not a tower.

From 1978 a series of excavations were carried out by the Department of the Environment, and a very different picture of the Castle emerged.

In the thirteenth century there was a hall house of substantial size, defended by a moat, probably before there were stone walls. Sufficient water runs down towards the burn on the south to supply a moat. The hall house is 100 feet in length and 30 feet in breadth. It has polygonal corner towers, which project 10 feet and are 15 feet in diameter. The N.E. tower had a spiral stair and one fragment of the N.E. tower stood to a great height. The basement was used for storage purposes and the residential apartments were on the upper floors. It compares in size to Haughton Castle, another hall house that had to be fortified. This came about at Edlingham from 1296 when William de Felton took over the property. He was prominent in the Scottish Wars of Edward I, and was one time constable of Roxburgh Castle. He became Sheriff of Northumberland. His son William was also involved in the warfare of the time. The manor house was fortified and a strong palisade erected inside the moat. A gatehouse was constructed as were some buildings in the courtyard, replaced by others at a later date. More substantial buildings date from the later fourteenth century.

In 1396 John de Felton died at Edlingham "where is a castle worth nothing by the year." It is not said whether this was the result of warfare. Elizabeth de Felton had married Sir Edmund Hastings of Roxby, Yorkshire, and he acquired the property.

Edlingham qualifies in 1415 as a castle and not just a 'fortalice'. The reason was that a keep had been added to the hall house, and this involved further alterations. The curtain walls had been rebuilt and strengthened. Courtyard buildings were improved, and the cobbled surface had been laid in the fourteenth century. The gatehouse was also extended and strengthened.

It seems that the tower was built over the moat that had been filled — a weakness that led to the split in the walls and vaulting of the basement.

The dimensions of the tower are 40 feet square with strong buttresses at each corner, which rise to support circular bartizans with battlements between them. Access to the roof and different floor levels was by a stair turret on the north side of the tower, between it and the hall house. There was a connecting building with a room above; holes for timbers can be seen. The stair turret ended with an umbrella vault and a look-out tower above the roof. At present it stands to a height of 50 feet, with no doubt splendid views, but the staircase has crumbled and only jackdaws can enjoy the heights.

In time of decay the south wall of the keep was broken and the basement was filled with fallen stonework to a height of ten feet. Before the excavations took place it was possible for cattle to walk in at first floor level and continue through the entrance of house, the remains of which were buried and overgrown. A hundred years ago when the relevant volume of the Country History was published, the writers only observed above this level. Recent excavations cleared the basement, discovering fragments of a trefoil window and the 7 ribbed springer of the umbrella vault. There was about half the ribbed vaulting of the basement tumbled here, the springers surviving on the north wall. Wide openings in the south wall and a mural chamber brought about the fall on this side. It is assumed that the slope was steep here and the Edlingham Burn flowed nearer than today, so that it was not liable to attack — certainly not by cannon.

The windows had very narrow openings, but were wide splayed to take seats, indicating with a fireplace that the basement was residential. There was a garderobe in the S.E. corner. The lintel of the fireplace was made of joggled masonry, like that of the fireplace above, which had fallen. The basement was entered through a door from the hall house at ground level, which was at some stage blocked. It had provided private and separate access to the courtyard, having an entrance protected by a portcullis with a vaulted chamber. The first floor in the tower contained a chamber that has been very much admired. It would "compare favourably, in point of detail, with any chamber of any other tower in the country". (N.C.H. Vol. VII P. 125).

It measures 22 feet square and 22 feet high to the crown of the vaulting.

It had two one light windows on the north side, possibly two on the east and south. The fireplace is 7 feet wide and had a joggled lintel. The brackets had sculptured heads, now much eroded. Two arched recesses in the west wall were connected with the draw well. The upper portion of the hall had a loft, probably reached by a ladder. There was a floor above the vaulting, but the upper level is impossible to interepret, since so much has disappeared. The tower was constructed in fine quality masonry and the completely surviving west wall gives a very good idea of this.

The excavations exposed the remains of a collection of buildings about the cobbled courtyard. The lower part of the hall house was put to farming usage and housing of animals at a later stage. The military emphasis tended to decline, but there was still a danger from cattle raiding.

There was an interesting incident at Edlingham in 1592. John Swinburne son of Thomas, married Anne, daughter of Sir Cuthbert Collingwood of Eslington, and in 1581 granted him use of lands, but reserving "the castle of Edlingham with the gardens and orchards". John Swinburne was a strong Catholic and wishes to disinherit his son, Thomas, who was a Protestant. Edlingham was said to be a haunt of Jesuits and in 1592 Sir John Forster sent a search party, but his men "found the walls of the late C14th castle so thick and the hiding places between the vaulting of the main hall and the floor above so numerous that 'traitors' could only be 'hungered out' after a more prolonged siege than they were prepared to conduct."

Pending an official guide by English Heritage visitors may find themselves similarly bemused by the complexity of the buildings. It does seem that there was an extension of the gateway to the north giving an extra gate, behind this was probably the moat crossed by a drawbridge (round holes for pivots can be seen in the masonry) which could be raised to block the entrance and a portcullis lowered behind.

There are signs of extended building to the north of the Castle, which may be the old village. The Norman Church on the way to the Castle is well worth a visit, especially since a defensive tower was added to the west end of the church, covering the original entrance. The tower, probably used by the priest and for a retreat, can only be entered through the church. Taken out of its church context it is exactly like the medieval border tower.

Edlingham passed to the Swinburnes of Capheaton, who suffered in the Civil War. Sir John Swinburne, returning from exile after 1660, destroyed Capheaton Castle to build Capheaton Hall. Edlingham Castle was used as a quarry for stone to rebuild the farm of Edlingham Newtown, which once had a tower. It seems that the stone was taken from the hall house and the courtyard buildings and not the tower itself, which did not suffer the final humiliation of Capheaton. A good deal of its history is now revealed in an area which is scenically fascinating.

Across the bleak moorland to the west of Edlingham and towards Rothbury there is little sign of habitation, and the first site of any importance is that of **Cartington,** which could be reached from Cragside by one of Lord Armstrong's carriage ways. Cartington was another of the castles that he took over and restored, but not for habitation.

It is situated on high ground overlooking the Coquet valley and is well supplied with water. It was a good defensive site and tenants for a long period were the family of Cartington. Their arms consisted of "three cart wheels silver". In 1441 John Cartington obtained a licence to crenellate his manor house at Cartington. In the early sixteenth century they were followed by the Radcliffes, and in 1601 Roger Widdrington obtained the property by marriage. He was a Catholic and friend of Lord William Howard: both were scholars and warriors. In 1648 the castle, which was held for the King, fell after a short siege, and serious damage was done to it.

The Castle has many stages of building and rebuilding, and the ruins are difficult to interpret, especially when overgrown in summer. When the first "castle" was begun by Thomas Lancaster (who built Danstanburgh), he did not ask for a licence. It seems to have been intended as a walled enclosure with 4 corner turrets, but the building was interrupted. Then the N.E. turret was replaced by a very substantial tower. It measured 45 feet by 33 feet with walls 8 feet thick. The basement was vaulted. This tower could have stood alone, but in the fifteenth century a hall and chambers wing was added to the west of the tower, taking over as part of the curtain. This was also barrel vaulted, and these were the buildings granted licence to crenellate in 1441.

By this time the Percies were the overlords of Cartington. The great tower had corner bartizans and in 1415 it was called "the turris" or tower of Cartington. In 1515 Queen Margaret of Scotland stayed a few days here, after giving birth to a daughter at Harbottle Castle. In 1541 it was described as "a good fortresse of two towers and other strong houses".

Roger Widdrington made additions and alterations. His grounds were described
"The Castle, houses, courtes, orchards & gardens, 3 acres".
New windows were inserted and a twin type roof given to the tower. A staircase tower was built and a new entrance was effected by steps to the first floor. Buildings were added on the eastern side of the court. The orchards and gardens were to the south of the buildings. It must have been made into an attractive residence, but the attackers in 1648 made a mess of it. The courtyard remained filled with debris to first floor level, when repairs were made in 1654.
Further restoration meant that in the reign of George I, Warburton described it — "Cartington: a handsome seat on the top of a hill".

By the early nineteenth century it was a ruin, and was later restored by Lord Armstrong as a landscape feature. This was faithfully done, but Cadwallader Bates did not like it.

The approach was through an enclosure to the west called the great forecourt and this leads to the forecourt with a Renaissance gateway at first floor level. The orchard to the south spilt over some of the ruins. Excavation of the forecourt showed the base for the stairs and the buildings to the east. To the north beyond the main buildings was the base court, of which part of the wall was traced. The south wall was rebuilt in the sixteenth century, partly over the S.W. turret, but the

Cartington Castle

Tosson Tower in ruins

Whitton Old Rectory - Pele tower on left

S.E. turret remains, probably covering an earlier entrance. There was another building to the east of the curtain wall. The vaulted basement of the great tower to the north was used as cellars and contained a well. The stair turret occupied the S.W. corner of this tower, which stands almost to full height. The first floor of the tower contained kitchen and buttery with service openings to the hall on the west side. The base of the hall range was vaulted and has been divided into separate apartments by later walls. A stair turret appears at the N.E. corner and the north wall was supported by a flying buttress. There was an entrance from the inner courtyard, and on this side part of the wall and upper windows remain.

Similarities in architecture have led to the suggestion that the architect of Warkworth was employed here. There are complicated stone stairs and little apartments with some frontal decoration as at Warkworth. The Percies were for a time lords of Cartington.

South of Cartington and close to the Coquet is **Thropton** tower, which still stands. In 1415 it was held by William Grene and in 1541 it was
"a little tower" of the inheritance of Sir Cuthbert Ratcliffe. It was capable of holding 20 men.

In the H.M.S.O. Survey it is called a bastle and had a vaulted basement. It was very strongly built with walls 5 feet thick, having 2 floors and an attic above. There was a doorway in the east end and both north and south walls show original first floor windows with holes for iron bars. It has been altered in course of time.

Further up the Coquet valley stand the ruins of **Hepple Tower.** This is mentioned in 1415 as a tower belonging to Sir Robert Ogle. While Thomas Lord Dacre was warden of the marches with a base at Harbottle, 20 men were stationed there, but had to be billetted houses since the Tower was not in good repair (1541).

In 1853 an account of it appeared in the Gentleman's Magazine —
"Hepple Castle is in the last stage of delapidation. About half a century ago the exterior walls of a strong & stately tower were still standing tolerably entire, which had probably been the manor house of the proprietors of Hepple . . . . until the Castle being ruined by the Scots, was totally abandoned by the lord, who removed his court to Great Tosson, where the tenants of Hepple & the demesne annually convene to this day. In erecting a few farmsteads an effort was made to demolish the remaining fragments of this strong tower, but the attempt after repeated trials, was relinquished by the workmen, who found it easier to cut stones from the hardest quarry than to separate them from the cement."
The tower had other buildings attached and dated to the fourteenth century. It measures nearly 40 feet by 30 feet with a vaulted basement. The walls are 6 feet thick. Since the vault is high there was probably another floor below the vault for storage. The entrance was by a south door into a lobby with stairs for two upper floors. It is likely to have been battlemented. It still stands in a ruinous condition with the vault partly fallen and the walls rather ragged.

On the other side of the river there was a tower at Bickerton, which has gone and another at Tosson which remains in a ruinous condition.

GREAT TOSSON TOWER

This was not mentioned in the 1415 survey, but it may well have been there. A century later it was in decay.
"At Great Tosson is a tower of Lorde Ogle's inheritance and not in good rep'ac'ons."
It was one of a series of fortifications guarding Coquetdale, and Tosson Burgh overlooking the valley was a prehistoric hill-fort. An extensive area here in medieval times was entitled Rothbury Forest, and there are extensive woodlands today.

The village of Great Tosson is some 500 feet above sea level with magnificent views over the Coquet Valley and the more distant Cheviots. It was a vantage point for detecting raiders or reivers. In 1517 William Ogle gave Tosson Tower to Lord Ogle in exchange for Cocklaw Tower near Chollerton on the North Tyne. Great Tosson Tower is now an interesting landmark. Vegetation has been cleared from the interior and old trees have been felled, making it much more visible. Yet it is strange in appearance — it has been much robbed for building stone, but the ashlar has been left at the higher levels, and the walls consist mostly of the core of rubble, so strongly built that they still stand. The original walls were some 9 feet in thickness, and the highest part stands to a height of 40 feet. This is the north east corner which has a doorway still standing and the top steps of a spiral stair. There would have been a turret here and perhaps at the other corners, joined by a rampart walk. The external dimensions are 42 feet from east to west and 36 feet from north to south. It had a barrel vaulted basement and is very much stronger and better built than the so called bastles. That it has stood in decay so long is a tribute to the quality of construction. It doubtless had a barmkin, and a spring provides a ready supply of water.

Great Tosson village was once much more populous and Great Tosson Farmhouse was the Royal George Inn, indicating that there was coach and carrier traffic. It was much visited in the last century and today there are walks in the Forest and access to the Simonside Hills, frequented by climbers. To the west along the Coquet is Hepple Tower, and to the east is Whitton Tower, once the rectory of Rothbury. This is an area of prehistoric as well medieval fortifications. Mackenzie in 1825 describing Rothbury Forest says —

"The whole is now dotted over with solitary farmsteads from a quarter of a mile distant from each other. These houses or rather strongholds, are very old and are usually called Peels, as before observed, from the celtic word 'Pil', a moated fort. Here, however, they are called Bastile buildings. The walls are in general about 5 feet thick and the stones secured by strong cement, though sometimes mud has been used. The doors, which are low and narrow, are usually placed at the east end of the building: the jambs of stone, with holes to receive a strong wooden bar, by which means the door was barred and the cattle secured on the ground floor: the light was admitted by loop holes.

The second floor is supported either by a stone arch or thick oak joists and was entered on the south side by stone steps, the door being fastened as below."

Continuing along the Coquet, we come to **Whitton Tower,** the fortified rectory of Rothbury. The original tower dates back to the fourteenth century, and in 1415 it was recorded as being in the possession of the Rector. It is unusual that being built into a hillside, the north wall rises to a height of 60 feet, while the south wall rises to 40 feet. The builder used the slope to get a sufficient supply of water. The vaulted basement measures $27\frac{1}{2}$ feet by $13\frac{1}{2}$ feet internally. The entrance is through two doors in the north wall, which is $9\frac{1}{2}$ feet thick. There is a well inside and the vaulted roof rises to a height of 12 feet. This is pierced by a manhole $2\frac{1}{2}$ feet square at the south end — the only inside way to the first floor above. This also has a stone vaulted roof, and the entrance on the east side is at ground level. A spiral stair occupies the S.E. corner of the tower. The south part of the vault was made into a study with a window through the 9 feet thick wall. The second floor provided sleeping accommodation, and a window recess was probably used as an oratory. The original tower had battlements, but the present ones are restoration.

In 1541 the report was —

"at Whytton nere unto Totheberye is a toure and a lytle barmekin being the manc'on of the p'sonage of Rothbery & is in good rep'ac'ons."

Sometimes the Rectors were non-resident and the buildings were neglected. A report of 1663 relates that there was a long house next to the tower containing a barn and byer. There was a little stackyard and a garden. The the north was an "old Courtan wall" making an enclosure.

In 1679 the Rev. John Thomlinson wrote

"At my coming to Rothbury . . . The parsonage house, besides its darkness and smokyness, not to be endured had (for want of covering to keep it dry) all the wood of it perfectly rotten, the floors as well as that which belonged to the roof & to say nothing of the stable etc. actually lying in their ruins."

He and Archdeacon Sharp later carried out repairs and extensions. The Archdeacon after 1720 was responsible for building another tower high in the gardens, commonly called "Sharp's Folly". It is a round tower 30 feet high and quite a landmark. Work was provided for the unemployed; and the Archdeacon could survey the sea, the stars, the landscape and his own people across the river in Rothbury.

Moving eastwards and south of the Coquet, the next fortification was **Eshot Castle,** now alas some humps and hollows in a field north of the Hall. In 1310 Edward II granted a licence to Roger Mauduit to crenellate his dwelling house at Eshot. In 1377 the manor and vill of Eshot were sold to Sir John Heron. In 1415 the list of fortalices records the "castrum de Eshete", belonging to Sir John Heron. This would indicate that it was larger than the ordinary tower. Later by marriage it became the property of William Carr, son of Thomas Carr and Elizabeth Heron. Little is known about the castle, but it seems to have been used to provide building material for the later hall at Eshot. It was surrounded by a moat and wall, and seems to have been rectangular with corner towers. Only excavation can reveal the details of size and strength.

Still further eastwards and overlooking the sea was **Widdrington Castle,** which has suffered the same fate as Eshot. The place, near the church, is marked by uneven ground and a group of trees called 'the twelve apostles'. In 1341 Gerald de Widdrington was granted a licence to crenellate his mansion by Edward III.

In 1415 Sir John Widdrington held the Castles of Haughton, Swinburne, Beaufront and Widdrington, so that he had an important part in border defences. The best impression of what the Castle was like is to be found from Buck's print of 1728, when it was part of a much larger building. It looks very much like Belsay of the same time. It had battlements and corbelled towers on the corners and was built in the same style, but windows had been inserted and other buildings added in course of time. In Elizabeth's reign Sir Robert Carey, who married a Widdrington widow, was frequently at the Castle. He was warden of the Middle Marches for a time, and when he was carrying the news of Elizabeth's death to James VI of Scotland, he stayed there. When James I made his way into England, he called at Widdrington and was refreshed. He also enjoyed himself hunting deer in the park, killing two.
"The game being so faire before him he could not forbear, but according to his wonted manner forth he went & slew two of them, which done, he returned with a good appetite to the house, where he was most royally feasted and banketted that night". April 8-9 1603.

Lord Widdrington was involved in the 1715 rebellion and was pardoned, but suffered the confiscation of his estates. The castle and other buildings fell into decay. Sir John Warren had them pulled down, and later when asked for a plan to build a house, he was provided with Buck's print of the old house. The mansion he built was destroyed by fire in 1776 and was replaced by a Gothic Folly.

South of Widdrington on the coast, **Cresswell Tower** survives. The mansion house next to it was demolished and the great hall built further away in the early nineteenth century has also been demolished. It is now the site of a caravan park; and the Tower is threatened by vandals. It measures 42 feet by 29 feet externally and 32 feet by 18 feet internally. The basement is barrel vaulted, and the two floors above are reached by a spiral stone stair. There is a turret at the N.E. angle, and the tower was battlemented. A much worn inscription on the turret window was supposed to read "William Cresswell, brave hero". Hodgson thinks this refers to William Cresswell, who died in 1698 and rebuilt the old hall adjacent to the tower.

COCKLE PARK is to the west of Cresswell, and the Tower stands high among the buildings of the Newcastle University Agricultural Experimental Station. It measures 60 feet by 36 feet at the north end, where the oldest part seems to be. This projects 9 feet wider than the mansion house and carries corbelled turrets with a machicolated parapet. There is a spiral staircase in the S.E. corner of the tower. On the east front of the tower is a large stone tablet that once carried the arms of Ogle and Bertram. Hodgson gives the date of the tower from this and a window with tracery as 1461. The window was later transferred to Bothal Castle.

There was probably an older manor house on the site, and old foundations have been discovered. The west side of the tower shows classical type windows of the Tudor period that have been blocked. The other side had Gothic type windows that were inserted later and weakened the structure. The building stands three floors high and had a parapet walk at the north end. It was in a dangerous condition, but has recently been repaired. The Ogles and Bertrams, who intermarried were both powerful families along the Wansbeck and Blyth valleys.

Hodgson mentions at Tritlington, to the north
"its chief curiosity is the old stone built mansion of the Threlkelds" with walled gardens and ornamented gates," but no date is given.

The Ogles built a house at Causey Park in 1589, which contained two circular stone staircases and it has been considered to have embodied a tower. Catherine Ogle of Causey Park was buried in Bothal Church May 23. 1609.

BOTHAL

Bothal, as its name indicates, was an Anglo Saxon settlement and there was probably an early church. In Norman times here was a suitable site for a Castle on a rising mound north of the Wansbeck, which covered a river crossing. If there was a motte, it has disappeared beneath the later gatehouse tower. There is no masonry visible earlier than the thirteenth century, but it was an early Castle.

It came to William Bertram, baron of Mitford, by marriage, and in 1212 Robert Bertram held it of the King by the service of three knights. In 1343 a licence was granted by Edward III to another Robert Bertram to make a castle of "mansum suum de Bothole". Sir Robert was one of twelve northern knights who won the thanks of the King for their bravery at the battle of Neville's Cross in 1346. The King was honoured on the walls of the great gatehouse built at Bothal at this time.

It is like Dunstanburgh, but in a different style, showing the desire of the baron to dominate the establishment.

The main bulk of the gatehouse measures about 40 feet by 30 feet. On either side of the gate a semi-octagonal turret extends 15 feet beyond the entrance and 3 feet outwards beyond the east and west walls. The entrance faces north and there is a fine ornamental window to the second floor. The gatehouse rises high, and is made very striking by a series of ornamental shields — perhaps an honour to Bothal and the knights who bore these arms. Pride of place went to Edward III, whose shield carried the three lions of England and the Fleur-de-Lys of France, showing his claim to that crown. The Black Prince is on his right and Lord Wake of Lydel in Cumberland on his left. Others in order were Aton of Alnwick, Greystock of Morpeth, Percy of Alnwick, Bertram of Bothal, Darcy, Conyers and Felton of Edlingham. On the west turret were Delaval, Scargill, Horsley and Ogle. In the reign of Edward III there was great stress on the ideals of knighthood and chivalry as in the stories of King Arthur. Edward III himself established the Noble Order of the Garter. "Honi soit qui mal y pense". The gatehouse had curious gargoyles and stone figures on the roof, one holding a horn and the other holding a stone in the act of throwing.

The gatehouse had a strong outer gate with portcullis and covered from the turrets above. The main passage was 33 feet long and 12 feet wide, vaulted in stone with three openings or "murder holes" in the crown, which could be used either to greet attackers or service the floors above. On the ground floor there were apartments in the turrets and within the walls behind. They included a porter's lodge and a prison. The spiral stone stair was in the south west corner, and there was another gate at this point to close the tunnel entrance.

The Great Chamber above this measured 25 feet by 20 feet, later divided by a partition. The garderobes were in the thickness of the wall to the south east. In the mid nineteenth century when the Duke of Portland was restoring the Castle a fine decorated window and fireplaces were installed from Cockle Park Tower on the same estate. There was another floor above this, later divided into bedrooms, and the spiral stair finished with an umbrella vault as in several other castles. It is thought that the same masons were here as at Prudhoe Castle. Above was the roof and the battlements — the merlons of masonry were twice as wide as the embrasures (openings) which were filled with shutters. Some round hinge holes can still be seen in the masonry. Archers would lift shutters quickly to fire, then letting them close against a reply.

The bailey or courtyard extends some 60 yards south from the gatehouse and towards the river. The curtain walls followed the contours and each side has a steep slope. Within this enclosure were a number of buildings that have disappeared. These were mentioned in a survey of 1576, when Lord Ogle owned the Castle.

"To this manor of Bothoole belongeth ane castell, great chaulmer, parler", 6 bed chambers, a gallery, buttery, pantry, larder, kitchin, bakehouse, brewhouse, a stable, a court "called the yethouse, wharin there is a prison, a proter lodge and diverse faire chaulmering, an common stable & a tower called Blanke (Blanche) Toure: a gardine, ane nurice, chapel and a toure called Ogles Toure & a pastre with many other prettie beauldings here not specified, faire gardings, & orchitts wharin growes all kind of herebes & floures, & fine appiles, plumbes of all kynde, peers, damsellis, nuttes, wardens, cherries, to the black & reede, wallnuttes and also licores verie fyne worth by the yeare £20."

Hodgson reported "of all these, only the gateway remains & the outer walls, sadly shattered & inclosing about 2 roods of land, scattered with fragments of buildings."

The gateway had a shed built against it. The north turrets were 53 feet high and the S.W. turret at the top of the stair was 60 feet high. He thought of the good old days, when hospitality was enjoyed there with music and rejoicing. He would be pleased that the Castle was restored by the Duke of Portland — to which Bates gave grudging admiration. At the present day the Castle is leased to Welwyn Electronics, and hospitality is provided in rooms that have a Tudor flavour. One picture shows Bernard Gilpin, the Apostle of the North, ending a quarrel in Rothbury Church. The old church of Bothal has considerable interest, and three quarters of a mile upstream was the Chapel of Our Lady, now reduced to ruins.

Bothal is an attractive village and Grose wrote —
"the banks of the Wansbeck, between this place & Morpeth, afford a variety of Sylvan scenes, equal in beauty to any in the kingdom."

Morpeth

The barony of Morpeth was granted by the King to William de Merlay, and in 1095 a castle was there, when Rufus (William II) "took Morpeth a strong castle". It stood on a hill, a modified natural mound, south of the River Wansbeck. This early castle was of earth and timber. There is no reason to think that there was a stone castle on this site called Ha' Hill.

In 1138 Ranulph de Merlay founded Newminster Abbey, and eight monks from Foundations stayed at his castle while monastic buildings were set up. During the twelfth century the castle was transferred to its present place across the burn to the south, perhaps taking over part of the settlement for this purpose. Stone curtain walls are said by Hodgson to date back to this time.

The Castle was destroyed in 1215 by King John and his mercenaries in his anger against northern barons, who had opposed him. After this the Castle was reconstructed, and the present gatehouse dates to the fourteenth century, by which time it belonged to Lord Greystock (hence his arms on Bothal Castle). The gatehouse tower controlled the entrance to the bailey which was surrounded by curtain walls. The slopes to both north and south of the Castle were steeper before the burns on either side were partly filled. There was a barmkin area to the east of the gatehouse, which today has the ruined walls of a barn.

A map of 1604, drawn for Lord William Howard when he took over the property from the Dacres, shows a strong tower and other buildings within the area of the bailey. The lords of Morpeth were mostly non-resident, and so the Castle was not kept in good repair. It was severely battered in the siege of 1644, during the Civil War. Pock marks from cannon balls can still be seen on the gatehouse tower.

It was restored by Earls of Carlisle for their agents, and in recent times has come into the hands of the Borough Council. Again it has suffered from time and neglect, needing further restoration.

On April 30th 1987, Mr Richard Branson visited the Castle to promote an environment scheme (U.K. 2000) for restoration by the British Trust for Conservation Volunteers. The gatehouse and walls will be repaired, and excavations may reveal the layout of abandoned buildings.

We think of Castles as residences of Lords and Barons, who in their time dispensed justice and kept prisoners. Lord Dacre kept prisoners at Morpeth at the Castle or the place that became the Old Gaol.

In the 1820s there was a grand scheme to build a new County Gaol and Court at Morpeth, below the old Castle. The architect, John Dobson, had made a special study of castles, including the Welsh constructions of Edward I. His Gaol was built on a Castle plan, with extensive curtain walls within which were the prison apartments. The Courthouse was the gatehouse, to guard entrance and exit, to decide who stayed and who departed. All kinds of work was done within, and a tread mill replaced the horse mill of the old castles. Some inmates remained for a long time, a few escaped and some went to the gallows.

Most of the prison buildings have been demolished, but the Courthouse still stands, a fine example of castellar structure, now used as residences and a restaurant. So all three Morpeth castles of different ages are separated, unlike others where different period structures are all on the same site.

Leland, in the reign of Henry VIII, wrote —
"Morpet a market towne is XII long miles from Newcastle. Wansbeke a praty ryver rynnithe thrwghe the syde of the towne. On the hethar syde of the river is the principall churche of the town. On the same syde is the fayre castle standing upon a hill, longing with the towne to the Lord Dacres of Gilsland. The towne is long and metely well buylded with low howyzys, the

stretes pavyed. It is a far fayrar towne than Alenwike."

He went on to mention Newminster Abbey, which had been dissolved and further along the Wansbeck —
"There be ruines of a castle longynge to the Lord Borow at Mydforde on the south syde of the Wansbeke . . . It was beten downe by the Kynge."

He does not say which King, which was King of the Scots.

MITFORD CASTLE

Mitford Castle was the head of barony, held in 1100 by William Bertram, who had married the daughter of Guy of Balliol. Mitford, therefore, was an early castle of the motte and bailey type. The site was well chosen, situated on a rocky ridge south of the Wansbeck, which curves round from the west and passes the east of the castle, where was one of two entrances. The Castle guarded the place of a ford, and later a bridge called Foss Bridge. The Park Burn comes into the area from the west, curving round the eastern side of the Castle and supplying a moat that surrounded the area, except the river side. The ridge was modified to take the Castle, so that ditches were dug and upcast carried to both sides. The motte occupied the highest point of the ridge with the bailey to the west and another enclosure called the barmkin to the east. The main entrance was at the west end of the Castle, but its nature cannot be determined since this area was used as a quarry for building Mitford Hall. The original Castle was of the earth and timber type, later replaced by stone structures.

In 1215-16 it was visited by the mercenaries of King John who laid waste the North, burning castles and towns. Mitford does not seem to have suffered badly, for in 1217 it held out successfully against the King of the Scots. Roger Bertram recovered the Castle from Henry VI, but his son died without male heirs.

Mitford was conveyed to John d'Estouteville, who sold it to the Earl of Pembroke in 1315. It was at this time that Sir Gilbert Middleton took over the Castle, and used it as a centre for pillaging. In 1317 he and his associates captured two Cardinals, Bishop Beaumont of Durham and his brother at Rushyford. The Cardinals were released, but the Bishop and his brother were imprisoned at Morpeth and Mitford Castles until ransoms were paid.

Later Mitford Castle was taken by a ruse and Gilbert Middleton was captured, tried and put to death. One of Gilbert's associates, Sir Walter Selby recovered the Castle with Scottish help. The Scots were making frequent forays at this time. The Castle has suffered severely and in 1327, then the property of Earl of Atholl, it was described as "the site of a castle wholly burned."

It was not habitable and useless for defence. In 1556 Lord Burgh sold Mitford lands to Cuthbert Mitford, but kept the Castle which was not obtained by the Mitfords till 1666. The same family now own the Castle and the Hall across the river, built by John Dobson, for which the Castle site was plundered for stone.

The Old Manor House, near the Church, succeeded the Castle as a residence. The Castle was made into a romantic ruin that could be viewed from the new Hall and the enclosure was converted into orchard and gardens. There exists a plan of 1810, drawn for Bertram Mitford, which gives a good idea of the ruins then before extensive quarrying. In more modern times the site became completely overgrown with trees and bushes. Vandalism helped natural decay and though some excavations were carried out before the war, they were never properly reported and the finds were lost. Mitford Castle is one of those places that should be taken over by English Heritage and properly excavated, since in a number of ways it is unique.

In the twelfth century the motte was converted into a shell keep — that is a stout wall surrounding the area within which buildings were constructed. The plan of 1810 shows only the west wall remaining with fragments elsewhere. Within the Castle area this inner ward was protected by a deep ditch. The doorway on the east side has survived, but much stone has been carted away from the shell keep wall. Foundations of buildings can be seen in the south west corner; and on the west front can be seen an arched opening which may have given access to a balcony. In the thirteenth century a stone keep was built within the shell keep and its shape was an irregular pentagon. It is said to be the only example of a five sided keep in England

"and it can hardly be doubted that the object of this peculiar device was to give the defenders better command of the angles of the tower which were exposed to attack from the inner ward." (Hamilton Thompson P.167). Access was by stone stair to the first floor, but only the double vaults of the basement now remain. These are eerie to explore since they were used as

Cockle Park Tower

Stanton Tower

Longhorsley Tower

prisons. One captive has carved the words "captives morior" (I die a prisoner.) Gilbert Middleton kept his captives here. Its use was properly a store and cellar. There were spouts to admit water, which could be collected.

The curtain wall on the east side of the keep has disappeared as far as the postern gate and its tower. The wall connected with the south side, where there was another mural tower. Here the wall stands to a considerable height, and is pierced by an opening with a semi-circular head. It overlooks a deep ditch, cut when stone was quarried to build the walls. The south west end of the site was already being quarried when the plan was made.

The gatehouse had disappeared, but the site of a chapel was marked and a bastion was shown on the west wall. Hodgson related that a lot of human bones were found during the quarrying and he thought it might record some massacre — it was more likely to be a cemetery. The west curtain wall still stands and one section shows rebuilding of a gap with larger stones, probably in the fourteenth century and there is no later stonework. There are no walls remaining round the outer bailey or barmkin. The Castle seems not to have been restored after 1327 when it was "wholly burned".

The pre-war excavations of 1938-9 uncovered the postern, which was 7½ feet wide. There was a beam socket for a bar and evidence of a portcullis. Excavations between the pentagonal tower and the shell keep revealed a rectangular building rather like Dally Castle, but digging down 5 feet did not reach the floor. It was suggested that this building preceeded the pentagonal tower, which partly covered it. It had walls more than 3 feet thick and was 23 feet wide — its full length could not be determined at the time. It was also revealed that there had been a church of cruciform shape and other buildings, built over buildings and a graveyard. Where burials had interfered with the foundations, builders had put the bones into new trenches. The graves were considered to be early; some just stone boxes and some had little headstones. Others were covered by long slabs. The skeleton in one grave was of a man wh measured 6 feet 2 inches in height — a medieval giant.

The "finds" were housed in a hut on the site. This became a war casualty and so the evidence has disappeared. In recent years elm disease has caused havoc among the trees covering the site, making them unattractive but revealing more of the Castle ruins. The Castle is private property, but can be visited by permission of the farmer or owner. It is now 660 years since it was burnt and surely deserves to become "English Heritage".

A mile or so west of Mitford and near Lightwater is the shrunken village of Newton Underwood. At the east end is an old farmhouse, which Hodgson called "Old Walls".

"At the north east corner of it is a garden containing an ancient arch of 12 feet span & built on walls 6 feet thick". There are other remains of foundations and local people told him that it had been a "bassel-house".

LONGHORSLEY

Hodgson went on to consider Longhorsley, several miles to the north, which had a Tower, and this still stands in the centre of the village and is something of a landmark. Adjacent to it is a Roman Catholic Chapel. The Anglican church, half a mile south of the village, is in ruinous condition and the old village school is used instead. The Tower belonged to the Horsley family and was built later than 1415.

It measures 42 feet from east to west and 30 feet from north to south. There is an entrance in the east wall, but an old square headed doorway in the south wall exists. This led into a vaulted basement 22 feet long by 18 feet broad. A door led into a gabled building added to the north in the seventeenth century. In the S.E. corner of the main building a wheel stair rises to three upper floors and the roof, which is battlemented. There was a latrine chamber in the N.W. angle of the second floor, concealed behind panelling that has been removed, and also a small mural chamber in the north east angle. The wheel stair ended with a small turret, which carried a bell. There is a walk around the battlements, from which fine views could be obtained of the village and the old deer park, which is the walled enclosure to the north of the Tower.

From the Horsleys, the Tower came into the inheritance of the Riddells of Swinburne and Felton. For many years the priest of the neighbouring chapel lived here. It is now a private residence.

Moving southwards by winding ways we reach Beacon Hill, which was a place from which warnings of raids were given, but could be used for ambush as for the Clavering, who fell not to the Scots, but to family rivals. Westwards are the Simonside Hills and immediately below the village of Stanton, where stands yet another tower.

Witton Shield Tower

Hepscott Tower

Harnham Hall Tower

STANTON

"Moderate alterations have so defaced the tower which John Corbet occupied in the time of Henry VI, that few traces of it are now observable: and the slashed and stone mullioned windows, put into it by the Fenwicks, are patched up with boards, or bundles of clouts and straw, or are open to the owls and daws. It is not, however, entirely tenantless. A person, who earns a livelihood out of its sunny and well walled gardens, lives in a part of it: a little shop is kept in another: a third portion of it is converted into a poorhouse; and the rest of its rooms are either unoccupied, or only occasionally used as granaries. Some of the rooms are wainscoted with high pannels and broad stiles painted an imitation marble; and others hung with tattered tapestry. Many of the offices and pent houses about it have been removed." Hodgson, writing in about 1830, said that there had been a chapel with burial ground and the village must in time past have been much larger. This is shown by the grass grown ruins of cottages and buildings.

In 1679 there were 45 "tenants within the manor". There was a good deal of coal mining in the area in the time of the Fenwicks and there were also lime-kilns, which can still be seen. Stanton Hall in the reign of Charles II was haunted by Veitch, the Covenanter, who also stayed at Harnham Hall. Both houses had hiding places for Non-conformists who were sought by the magistrates.

The building of Stanton is difficult to interpret because of many changes, but it is quite impressive. There is a stair turret, probably sixteenth century, which rises to four storeys in height. There are extensions to the east and the west with a variety of windows, some of which have been blocked. The extension to the west was eighteenth century, but it includes older stonework. There must have been many places for men like Veitch to hide. The Hall has been restored in recent times and it is a market gardening centre.

Witton Shield is within sight of Stanton, and stands upon high ground above the confluence of two burns. It has a strongly defensive position from the north, and the garden walls are a reminder of the old type of barmkin. The house is strongly built of local stone with thick walls. Large stone blocks form the quoins in bastle house style. Like Stanton it has a stair turret with a spiral stiar, and it rises to three storyes. Some of the small old windows have been blocked and replaced. Over the door is the date 1608 and the initials NT for Nicholas Thornton. NT is repeated on the inner door and high on the stair tower is a shield with the arms of Thornton impaling Ratcliffe. There was a Roman Catholic chapel there, and Hodgson reported stucco work on the ceiling.

Netherwitton. The elder branch of the Thorntons lived at Netherwitton or as it was then called Witton by the Waters. The Font provided water power for a cotton mill constructed for the Thorntons about 1780. The tower called Witton Castle was demolished when Netherwitton Hall was built by Robert Trollope about 1670. Some of the stonework from the old tower was incorporated in the new building on its north side. One tablet, from the old building, bears the date of Edward V 1483, one of the princes of the Tower. Netherwitton was close to the old Roman road called Devil's Causeway. Oliver Cromwell stayed at Netherwitton in 1651, when campaigning in Scotland.

Moving southwards over the Wansbeck, we approach Meldon where a tower once belonged to Nicholas Heron. The village stands on high ground overlooking a walled enclosure, which once was a deer park with a keeper's watch house. In the sixteenth Century Meldon became the property of the Fenwicks and Sir William Fenwick moved here from Hartington. In the church is his memorial (1652). A knight he reclines on his side, his hand to his cheek, probably part of a larger monument.

The tower and hall have gone, but Hodgson recorded the ruins in a field to the SE of the church. He found the remains of a strongly built vault measuring 60 feet long and 15 feet wide within the walls. There was a large covered sewer running northwards towards the river; and remains of other buildings with a barmkin. The orchard, gardens and groves had disappeared.

Present day Meldon Park is to the north of the Wansbeck, a classical mansion designed by John Dobson for Isaac Cookson in 1832.

The road here passes Temple Thornton and West Thornton, where there were a number of bastle houses. It was near the

Devil's Causeway, and Warburton (1718) thought it might be a Roman town. The Roman road crossed the river Hart at Hartburn, where there is a fine medieval church and a vicarage that started as a "vicar's pele". At the north end of the garden, Dr Sharpe erected another folly, designed to look like a battlemented medieval tower. From this could be seen Rothley Castle. The building was a school house and school room, delightfully situated and overlooking the river in its wooded valley.

Longwitton Hall, north of the Hart, may have been a tower. Hodgson wrote of a very thick wall within the Hall that may have been part of the mansion of the Fenwicks.

South of the Wansbeck again we see Bolam on a hill with the church and hall among the trees. On the hill top was a prehistoric promontory fort with double rampart and ditches, now covered with trees. Within this enclosure was the early castle, about 1100, the head of a barony.

In medieval times Bolam was a large settlement with some 200 houses, which have disappeared long ago like the castle. Hodgson went there when Mr. Horsley was building Bolam Hall. A lot of ruined walls were revealed, the stones reddened by fire. Much of the stone was re-used. He could make out the remains of a strong tower, measuring 40 feet by 30 feet. There were foundations of other buildings.

George Mark had written —

"There has been formerly a very considerable castle at the west end of this village. The fosse is very visible and has been of vast depth."

In Bolam Church is the legless effigy of Robert de Reymes of neighbouring Shortflatt Tower, which the church served with Harnham and Belsay. At these places the medieval towers have survived as well as the tower already mentioned at East Shaftoe. This is an interesting area for castles.

Harnham Hall is situated on an outcrop of rock north of the river Blyth. At one time there was a fortified village, now reduced to two farms and cottages. In 1415 there was a "turris" or fortalice belonging to Robert Swinburne. It was a much more strongly defensive place than Shortflatt and overlooked the Devil's Causeway, very much a medieval route to the Border and used by the Scots, since it connected with Dere Street.

Harnham Hall had a wide outlook and a beacon for warning of raids. Today the tower is not noticed; it is hidden behind the seventeenth Century hall. At other places along the Blyth as at Shortflatt or West Beechfield, the hall has been built to the east of the tower. At Harnham "at the back of the house high up a steep rocky bank and on a daring substructure, stands a medieval tower". (Pevsner).

After 1660 Major Babington, a Cromwellian officer, came to live with his wife Kate Haselrigg, the widow of Colonel Fenwick. Both Fenwick and Babington had been governors of Berwick. Kate Babington died in 1670, but being excommunicate, was not permitted to be buried in Bolam churchyard. She was buried in a rock cut tomb in the garden of Harnham Hall. The garden wall is decorated with double-faced statues, both male and female. Before her death Kate had cut into a pane of glass the words "Omnia vanitas" (All is vanity).

Shortflatt Tower is not far away in the fields on lower land. This, like Harnham, was part of the barony of Bolam. Between 1293 and 1295 it was acquired by Robert de Raymes, who also held Aydon. In 1296-7 Scottish armies came slaying and burning; both Corbridge and Hexham were burnt, and local lords had to look to their defences.

On April 5th, 1305, Reymes was given licence —

"to fortify or embattle his dwelling houses at Shortflatt and Aydon."

Shortflatt Tower was built as part of larger scheme of fortification. Raymes served in the Scottish Wars and may have been captured at Bannockburn. It was reported that Bolam and Shortflatt were burnt and the tenants fled. Aydon also suffered, and Raymes was practically ruined since he had to pay a ransom of 500 marks with his son kept as hostage. Robert died in 1324 and his land was worth nothing "owing to the destruction of the Scots."

His grandson, Nicholas, was involved in unlawful activities in conjunction with the Herons and several of them suffered imprisonment. Yet he became a Member of Parliament and one time warden of Roxburgh Castle.

Mitford Castle

Aydon Castle, built by Robert de Reymes

Shortflatt Tower, also built by Robert de Reymes

In 1450 Shortflatt was described as the site of the manor containing "a hall, 3 chambers, three cellars, one kitchen and divers other houses for husbandry which are worth nothing besides deductions because they are totally ruined by the destruction of the Scots and the laying waste thereof in the last war." In the sixteenth century danger continued and watches had to be kept. The sounding of the horn meant that local men must "rise and follow the fray".

In 1552 the overseers of the watch were Robert Raymes of Shortflatt, Robert Middleton of Belsay, Roger Fenwick of Bitchfield and John Horsley of Milbourne Grange. Raiders from Tynedale and Redesdale added to the disorder. In the early seventeenth Century Henry Raymes sold Shortflatt to William Selby, who added to the manor house.

The great tower is fourteenth Century and measures 34 feet by 20 feet internally with 6 feet walls, making external dimensions 46 feet by 32 feet. The basement is barrel vaulted rising to 11½ feet at the crown. All the openings have been modernised, both doors and windows. It has two other floors and an attic with a pointed roof; around the top are battlements and a parapet walk.

To the east of the tower is a hall or central block, some of which seems to date to the sixteenth Century. It is about 60 feet long and 25 feet wide, two stories high with a garret. Windows show different periods of alteration, and there is a great chimney. The house also contains a priest's hide-hole.

Hodgson's account is interesting. (1827)
"Shortflat, situated on flat ground, on the south side of a reedy brook, called Howburn, is a mansion house in the style of Queen Elizabeth's days, covered with a grey freestone slate and built against an old tower. The approach to it is by a doorway in the garden wall, finely overhung with ivy. The tower is of strong masonry and in good repair: its upper parts occupied by the farmer of the Shortflat grounds and its vault used as a cowhouse."

At this time it was purchased by John Dent and restoration made, which included the addition of a north wing. The same family of Hedley Dent still own the property and all the tower is used for residential purposes — cattle excluded from the precincts. The garden area was possibly the old barmkin.

Belsay Castle

"Belsay is one of the most impressive castles of Northumberland. It is also one of the most interesting to study." Pevsner.
"Belsay, with its traceried two lights opening on the first floor, and large bartizans corbelled out at the angles of its battlements, is the most handsome building of its kind in the north of England." Hamilton Thompson P.312
W. D. Simpson, another expert on castles, adds —
"perhaps the most impressive of them all."

It stands midway between Newcastle and Otterburn, and the Devil's Causeway was not far away, so that it was in a place of primary importance in communications with Scotland.

Belsay belonged to the Middletons, in royal service until the lamentable lapses of Edward II. Sir Gilbert Middleton was involved in kidnapping and raiding, so that he forfeited his life and property. Sir John de Strivelyn, a distinguished soldier and related to the Middletons, took over. There was a manor house at Belsay, but Sir John was responsible for the building of a magnificent Tower house. He served Edward III in his wars and was no doubt well versed in fortification. In addition he acquired something of the King's love of chivalry and display. The same characteristics have been noticed about the Percies and the same sort of display on the front of Bothal Castle. These were years of victory in Scotland and France. The gallantry and splendour of the time were recorded in Froissart's Chronicles. There was display in buildings, both castles and churches. A castle was something more than a grim fortress — it could be a comfortable and ornamental residence. "Among secular buildings, no better illustration of this 'arrogant splendour' — can be found than at Belsay Castle. It is the embodiment in stone and lime, of the fantastic chivalry, the uninhibited gaiety, of the third Edward's Court. In its own medium it expresses the same mood as the extravagant peace-time costume and the bizarre panoply on the field of war, with which the gallant band of warriors whom the brilliant king drew together at his Round Table, adorned their dignity of rank and set forth their pride of prowess. The very spirit of that far off time seems to be portrayed in the martial yet fantastic profile of the Belsay tower house." (W. D. Simpson)

Belsay appears to be square in plan, especially since the entrance was built over by a later building, hiding decoration, if there was any like the Bothal over the front. The entrance from the north is through a deep recess, overlooked by the projecting wings of the N.W. and S.W. towers. It was well covered against attack. The spiral staircase is in the south west tower. In the main part of the building there are three floors. The basement is vaulted and contains the well. It was used for storage and perhaps keeping some animals. Later a kitchen was here and in more recent times an entry was cut through the east wall, showing its amazing thickness and strength. On the first floor is the hall, well lighted by traceried windows with window seats at either end. The upper hall or solar was above, the corbels that took the timbers of the floor can still be seen.

There were fire places on both floors and perhaps surprisingly the hall was beautifully decorated with painting. some of this has been recovered by experts of English Heritage. Hodgson wrote —

"The walls of this room for 6 feet or more upwards have been ornamented with lozenge shaped chequers in distemper work; and for 3 further feet up with trees and armorial bearings, amongst which is one shield quartering Ogle and Bertram."
There were other armorials. One of the paintings recently recovered shows a medieval ship as well as the trees bearing armorial shields. This hall measures 43 feet by 21 feet and 17 feet high. The ribbed vaulting above the windows show that these too were painted, and the interior must have been very attractive.

In the S.W. wing containing the spiral stair there are six rooms, one above the other. The room level with the hall was the original kitchen with a serving hatch; and the fireplace occupied the space of what is now a window. When the kitchen was transferred to the basement, this room became an oratory. The top room of the six is above the battlements and is approached by an outside stair. The other wing contains four floors — the ground floor being a cellar, approached from the guard room entry. Above this is a private chamber with a garderobe and two apartments above.

The tower house measures externally 56 feet by 47 feet and rises to a height of 70 feet. Strong corbelled turrets crown the corners of the tower, each with a room and battlemented. The S.W. turret rises higher than the others and adds to the impressiveness of the buildings. A corbelled and machicolated parapet encircles the whole building, so that attackers at any part of the tower could be engaged.

The masonry deserves attention, and mason's marks and a change in the ashlar may indicate that there was an interruption in building, probably the result of the Black Death in 1348.
There are similar mason's marks at Chipchase and Cartington.
Looking again at Belsay Castle, we can echo Hodgson —
"the tower itself is certainly one of the most perfect, and by far the most imposing specimen of castellated architecture in Northumberland."

This is not all, however, Belsay was added to in the early seventeenth Century in a way that was harmonious. Some towers with halls stuck against them look odd, but not this. A hall was added to the west covering the entrance to the Castle, but containing a new columned portico of date 1614 "Thomas Middleton and Dorothy his wife built this house." On an ornamental tablet are the arms of Middleton and Strivelyn with "T.M. 1629".

The Castle is in a beautiful situation, and the old barmkin area was converted into gardens and parklands. In the eighteenth Century a west wings was added to balance the castle tower. Instead of a moat was a ha'ha and ornamental gardens.

From 1810-17 Sir Charles Middleton Monck built a new Belsay Hall in Greek style, away from the Castle, which remained habitable. The quarries were converted into gardens and the whole are landscaped. There are other buildings in the castle area — barns, stables and kennels and a "folly" on the hill.

"It has been combined with a landscape setting, deliberately designed to enhance it in a manner which makes this whole group of Belsay Castle, old and new, with its attendant lay-out of gardens and grounds, and the planned village outside the demesne, one of the most interesting manorial assembles to be found anywhere in England." W. D. Simpson.
It is all in the care of English Heritage and open to the public.

To the north of Belsay and on the river Blyth is Bradford, once a considerable village, witnessed by the unevenness of the land. There are now two farms, and the south farm has an interesting barn, which was in fact Bradford Hall belonging to the

Ogles. Inside there is a huge fireplace spanning the building, and inscribed on the lintel is G.O. 1567. This was Gilbert Ogle, and the building was an Elizabethan Hall. There is no sign of defence. The building measures 60 feet by 30 feet, and there is a dividing wall within, the east end being the byre. It is not vaulted, and there have been a number of changes with windows and doors blocked. The main part has been converted into a barn with wide doors, and it is impossible to see if there was a stair turret. Was this a return to the unfortified hall house? The earthworks to the west may be gardens and fishponds, but they have given scope to much fantastic speculation.

West of Belsay Castle and at the end of a rural road is Kirkheaton, a village once larger than it is. It had collieries and vast limestone quarries. The church is perched near one old quarry face and near it is the manor house. This is a Jacobean house of the Herons, and later used as a parsonage. It is attractive with a walled garden, and at the east end is a squarish eighteenth Century addition. This was built on the foundations and partly the walls of the medieval tower house. Part of the spiral stair is preserved in the structure. In olden times there were several tracks through this area and the Devil's Causeway passes close. Cromwell is said to have stayed at the manor house. Kirkheaton has a little disused Methodist Chapel as well as the Anglican Church.

At Blackheddon there is an old house of the Fenwicks with thick walls and an outside chimney, which carries the date 1614 on the doorhead. It has the appearance of a strong house, and like Meldon is said to be ghosted by a wraith called "Silky", from the sound of silken dresses.

To the west is Bitchfield Tower which goes back to the fifteenth Century. It is strongly built and barrel vaulted at the basement.

There is evidence from the stonework to indicate that it had corbelled bartizans on the corners. The garderobe has a modern lavatory installed. To the east of the tower, and attached to it, is a seventeenth Century mansion. A stone head of a blocked door carries the letters RF 1622 IF — Robert and Jane Fenwick.

The Fenwicks also had a Tower at **Ryal**, which has been replaced by a later building. Since the Roman Wall was not far away and the Devil's Causeway came near Ryal, Roman stone was used for buildings including the church.

There is yet another Tower of the Fenwicks at Fenwick; in 1415 it belonged to Henry Fenwick. The remains of the tower are embodied in a building at Fenwick North Farm. Here in 1775 a labourer, who was taking down part of the tower found a collection of 220 gold coins of the time of Edward III. It has been thought that this was to be a ransom for Sir John Fenwick's two sons, who were held prisoners by the Scots. The cache of coins was under the floor of the basement of the tower. On the other hand it may have been hidden away from raiders. Pevsner's cryptic comments are "Tower — crenellated 1378. Not very eloquent remains in a farmyard."

Stamfordham, the next village along the river Pont, had a vicar's tower in 1415; and the church has a strongly built square tower, entered only from within. It contains medieval monuments.

Ponteland also has a vicar's pele, which still stands in a grove of trees not far from the church. It is a rather gaunt looking building, almost disapproving of the rookery around it. Little is known about it, but the County History gives a picture, which makes it appear larger with additional buildings.

Ponteland had another tower, belonging in the fourteenth Century to the Earls of Atholl. In 1388 during the Douglas raid, which ended at Otterburn, Froissart tells us that it was attacked by the Scots.

"Then they ordained to assail the castle and gave it a great assault, so that by force of arms they won it and the knight within it. Then the town and the castle were brent."

Mark Errington rebuilt this tower at the beginning of the seventeenth Century as a family mansion. It is now known as the Blackbird Inn, and it is possible to drink in the vaulted basement of the old tower. Parts of the Jacobean mansion remain with later additions. It is an attractive building, and across the street is Ponteland Church with a Norman tower built from Roman stone.

Moving eastwards the next tower was at **Kirkley**, in 1415 belonging to Sir Matthew Eure. This was probably replaced by the Hall, built in 1632 for Cuthbert Ogle and Doroty Fenwick his wife. Their combined arms on a stone from this house, built into a later one, are all that remains, the hall being so much altered at different times. It now houses an Agricultural

College, and is situated south of the river Blyth, which is joined by the Pont. The Ogles were a powerful family with extensive lands.

Their next residence to view is **Ogle Castle,** which in 1415 belonged to Sir Robert Ogle. In 1341 Edward III had granted a licence to Robert de Ogle to crenellate "mansum suum de Oggle". He, in the same year, had captured five Scottish knights. He married Helen Bertram, and in due course Bothal was added to the Ogle heritage. Their son Robert was buried in Hexham Abbey in 1410.

In 1346, after the Battle of Neville's Cross, John de Coupland brought David Bruce, King of Scotland, as a prisoner to the Castle. The Castle has not been closely investigated by historians and might repay research. Today it is an L shaped building with the tower at the west end and the mansion house to the east of it. It was double-moated and parts of these remain in the trees to the west.

To the west is the deserted medieval village of Ogle.

Hodgson quotes from material presented to the Duke of Newcastle, who married into the Ogle family —

"albeit it is not large, yet it hath been a strong and handsome structure. Several towers were upon the wall built in a half moon outwardly and in a square within surrounded with a double moat and drawbridges before the gate, seated in as pleasant a soil as the country doth afford".

A print showing the castle rectangular with corner towers has been described as artist's imagination. However, it was rated as "a castle" in 1415, so it was much more than a tower.

In 1776 Hutchinson wrote —

"very little remains of the old castle; part of a circular tower adjoins the **east** of the farmhouse which stands on the site of the castle: the windows of this tower are very small, topped with painted arches, the whole remains carrying a countenance of very remote antiquity. The ground where the chief part of the castle stood is square, guarded by a double moat, divided by a breastwork of mason work. The walls are quite levelled to the ground and the moat almost grown up."

This was a century after the writing to the Duke of Newcastle.

Hodgson, in 1827, saw —

"the western end of the moat was still sharp and perfect where the rampart that divides the ditches is about 60 yards long."

To the east the ditches had been levelled for convenience of farming. He considered that the house was built as a country residence for Lord Ogle in the style of the time of Charles I.

"The great number of fireplaces and apartments which it contains, show that it was built for the reception of a considerable establishment."

North of Ogle and the river Blyth is **Whalton** with a fine medieval church. On the opposite side of the road is the old vicarage, which has a vaulted vicar's pele at the west end, one of many in Northumberland.

Blagdon, eastwards, had a tower, but this was replaced in the eighteenth Century by the Hall of the Whites and Ridleys. On the other side of the A1 and overlooking the river Blyth is Plessey Hall, which is defended on the north by the river and the west by a deep ravine. It also seems to have had deep ditches or moats. Today it is a farmhouse, with two periods of building. The older part has very thick walls.

Hodgson said that there were signs of much more extensive buildings and gardens, belonging to a time when it was held by the Widdringtons and protected by a wall and a ditch. There is a document of 1349 in which Roger de Widdrington undertook to build for Margaret de Plessey a house

"within the site of the manor of Plessys, to consist of a hall, a chamber, a pantry, a buttery, a brewhouse and a byre for 6 cows and their calves."

Hodgson thinks that this was not the manor house, but gives a good idea of a mansion of the time.

"The place is admirably chosen for retirement and security."

Eastwards along the river is Bedlington. Bedlingtonshire until 1844 belonged to the Bishopric of Durham, and was not included in the administration of history of Northumberland.

In Bedlington north of the church was **Bedlington Old Hall,** with a medieval tower attached to it. The buildings were demolished in recent years, and were replaced by the present Council Offices in Front Street.

Along the Wansbeck there was a tower at Choppington, which "was buylded by Gawen Ogle" about 1503. This has disappeared and the so-called "castle" at Hirst has also gone.

At Hepscott there is an old tower, attached to a house of a later period. Hodgson gives little about it "an old hall, which was a tower and has had additions lower than itself made to it and the whole roofed in at the same pitch, which gives it an old appearance."
These extra buildings and an overgrowth of ivy make it very difficult to interpret.

Southwards over the Blyth river, the next place with a fortification was **Horton**. In 1415 it was "Castrum de Horton iuxta mare" i.e. Horton by the sea; and held by William de Whitchester. It was Delaval property. In 1292 Sir Guischard de Charron entertained King Edward I in his manor house at Horton, and obtained a licence to crenellate from the King. Sir Guischard was an itinerant justice and often stayed at his manor house here. The property was gained by marriage. Work began immediately on fortification and we hear about the construction of the moat or ditches. Guischard's son was also a justice and a warrior, being killed at Bannockburn in 1314. Horton was later taken over by Sir Gilbert Middleton's supporters, and in 1318 Walter de Selby and others held out in a siege. It gives the impression that Horton Castle was quite important, but it is now no more.
In 1909 Volune IX of the County History gave a plan of farm buildings surrounded by a moat, which was 33 feet wide. In 1947 I only remember the moat on the south side which was called a "duck pond". The area within the moats was about 200 feet square. There was said to be a double moat like Ogle Castle, but the outer moat was not visible. The old castle was dismantled in 1809 and the stone was used to erect farm buildings within the enclosed area. Horton has extensive views over the sea; and the Old Plessey Waggonway passes by — down to Blyth Harbour. The tower of Weetslade, mentioned in 1415, has also disappeared, and has not been located.
The **Castle of Seaton Deleval** has suffered a similar fate. In 1415 Sir William de Wychester held the "Turris de seton de la vale", and there is very little information about it. Hutchinson said that it stood near the Hall that was built to the designs of Vanburgh in the first half of the eighteenth century.

Some information can be obtained about the old hall from the Delaval records. An inventory of 1606 lists goods and chattels in the great bedchamber, the parlour, the great dining chamber with kitchen, larder and buttery. Sir Ralph Delaval, who died in 1628,
"builded the long new house at Seaton to the garden wall of the grounds, the brewing house, the crosse house betwixt the tower and the gardner . . . He builded a new baking house and part of the kitchen".
He set battlements on the front of the house and built walls all about it. The forecourt was flagged and other buildings were added. New windows were put in and panelling in some of the rooms. But the family fortunes faltered, and in 1718 Admiral Delaval bought a sadly decayed establishment.

He decided to have a new building in the grand style.
"Vanburgh preferred to lay out his mansion on new lines. Work commenced in 1720 with the complete demolition of the old tower and hall, and continued to be carried on slowly during the next eight years."
Vanburgh's Hall still stands despite the ravages of fire and time. It can be visited on Wednesday and Sunday afternoons in summer. (May 1—September 30).

A reminder of the medieval past is the Norman chapel of Our Lady at Seaton Delaval, which is close to the Hall. It contains the effigies of a medieval knight and his lady — either Sir Eustace Delaval who died in 1258 and his wife, Constance de Balliol; or Sir John Delaval, who died in 1272 and his wife, Mary de Biddleston.

A tower that still stands can be seen at **Burradon,** south of Cramlington. It is small, measuring 25 feet by 22½ feet and rises three stories in height. The stonework is rough rubble with large well cut quoins. At roof level can be seen the remains of a parapet carried on corbels. There is machicolation over the entrance on the east side. The basement is vaulted and it has a spiral stone stair. A fireplace on the first floor carried the initials L.O. (Lancelot Ogle) 1633. The walls have fallen on the sides weakened by having larger windows than usual in a tower of this type.

Ogle Castle

Cambo Tower

Tynemouth Castle

There was a tower at Seghill in 1415, which belonged to William de la Val. The only remains of it were in the basement of the Blake Arms Hotel. Its walls were four feet thick; and the internal measurements were 40 feet long by 16½ feet wide within a vaulted basement. It was three stories high and had a turret on one corner. There was a door at first floor level approached by external steps, and indications are that it was quite a large tower.

In 1415 there is recorded the "Turris de Whitle iuxta Tinmowth" and this belonged to the Prior of Tynemouth. Before it developed as a seaside resort Whitley was notable for coalpits and limestone quarries. The tower has disappeared without trace, but there are substantial remains at **TYNEMOUTH.**

Here the rocky headland was used in Saxon and Roman times. When the Normans came it was the site of a castle as early as 1095, when it listed a siege of two months before being taken by William Rufus. In 1296 Edward I gave the prior a licence to crenellate. The situation was serious with Scottish attacks and Hexham Priory was destroyed.

The Tyne was a necessary part of the defence of the Kingdom and Tynemouth concerned the King directly. In 1297 Tynemouth's defences were sufficient to discourage the Scots from attacking, though the Priory housed the valuables of the inhabitants of the town. Edward I and Edward II were often at Tynemouth, since the Priory provided hospitality and the castle provided defence for the Priory.

With Sir Robert Delaval in charge, the castle held out against Gilbert de Middleton's supporters. In 1346 Sir William Douglas, invading England, sent word to Prior Thomas de la Mare to prepare dinner for him. He came, but not as he anticipated. Defeated at Neville's Cross with King David, who was also captured, Douglas came as a prisoner. Ralph de Neville, who had charge of the Castle, had him sent there. Prior Thomas later became Abbot of St. Albans; Tynemouth was a dependency of that abbey. In 1390 King Richard II was persuaded to give £500 for the repair of the Castle, and other barons subscribed too.

The gatehouse was put into the form that can still be seen today. Tynemouth Priory was frequently visited by people of importance, since there was access by sea as well as by land. Hospitality could be very expensive and both the Priory and Castle needed repairs.

When the Priory was dissolved in 1539, it had 15 monks and a few novices. Its wealth, buildings and extensive lands were taken over by Henry VIII. The King's advisers realised a royal fortress was needed here. Sir John Lee reported — "a place so nedeful to be fortified as none within the realm more." He had the advice of Italian experts, and in 1545 a thousand men were employed. £2,633" 4" 3d was spent mostly on wages, since stone was at hand. Outworks were built on the landward side and batteries were set up. Thirteen hundred Spanish troops arrived in Newcastle for the King's service, and some were stationed at Tynemouth.

In 1557 the Earl of Northumberland leased the site of the Priory, and Sir Henry Percy became captain of the Castle. Some repairs were made since it was realised that the Castle was necessary for the defence of the Tyne and against danger from the sea. Sir Henry Percy did not join the Rising of the North in 1569, and held the Castle for the Queen. He received his brother's estate later in 1576, but was involved in conspiracy. He was deprived of Tynemouth which was not properly maintained. Since there was danger of foreign invasion, Robert Carey was put in charge. The Earl of Huntington was ordered to act "for the better defence of the castle of Tynemouth and that coast". He replied that there was a lack of men and munitions at both Tynemouth and Newcastle. Fortunately the Armada was defeated at sea in 1588; and there was the continuing story to the end of Elizabeth's reign and beyond that the Castle was neglected. It has played a part in military matters. While the Priory church was used by the parish, the precincts were used by troops. Monastic buildings were converted to their use. It is only in recent years that troops are no longer there, except for mock battles on a site under the care of English Heritage and open to the public at all times.

The approach to the Castle site explains the choice of place. A promontory juts out into the sea with three sides of steep rocky cliffs. On the western side a deep ditch was cut to complete the circle of defence. It is not certain if there was anything of this before Mowbray's time, but it would carry a strong timber stockade and other impediments on the slopes. On the inside of the moat another rampart of earth was built up and on the south side of this overlooking Prior's haven was what was called the "mount" or motte.

This later provided access to the gatehouse at first floor level. Edward I's licence meant that the whole area could be defended by curtain wall, battlements and towers. The gatehouse covered a raised causeway which was the way to the Castle, but it became ruinous and was restored in 1390 with the same defensive ideas as at Dunstanburgh or Bothal.

The new gatehouse was an oblong tower with a projecting barbican as at Alnwick. The tower measures 56 feet by 35 feet — 4 stories in height. The barbican stretches 54 feet outwards with an open courtyard and then a completely covered part 38½ feet by 34 feet.

The entrance was protected by gates and portcullis with vaulted guard chambers on either side. There were chambers on two stories above, including one for the working of the portcullis. A spiral stair connected the barbican with the gatehouse Tower. Between them was a pit, as at Alnwick, to take a drawbridge. This covered the arched passage through the basement of the gatehouse which had guardrooms and inner gates, covered by machicolation at second floor level. The gatehouse was entered from the east by a door at first floor level, which also had a drawbridge. In the gatehouse proper at this level is the Great Hall and in the "Mount Chamber" is the adjoining kitchen. Above the Great Hall was the Great Chamber and above were the battlements. At each corner of the gatehouse tower was a corbelled turret or bartizan as at Belsay.

In front of the Mount the medieval curtain wall was replaced by earthworks revetted in stone to carry artillery. This was done in Elizabethan times as at Berwick. The triangular earthwork projecting in front of the barbican was in the same style. South of the Mount is a surviving stretch of medieval wall and the rectangular 'Mount Tower'. There is another stretch of wall with a medieval semi-circular tower and down the cliff the tower by Priors Haven. Beyond this the wall has disappeared. On the north side of the enclosure beyond the gun platform is the medieval Whitley Tower at the NW angle and sections of the medieval walls still remain here.

The waves echo in Jingling Geordie's Hole, said to be the hide of a wrecker. This promontory has witnessed a great deal — the coming of ships throughout the ages, storms, wrecks and the emergence of life boats. There are the monastic ruins and the story of the church with an extensive graveyard. On the other side of Priors Haven was the Spanish Battery of the Elizabethan period and a monument to Admiral Collingwood, hero of Trafalgar. South Shields Roman Fort is across the river.

NEWCASTLE

The river Tyne was for the greater part of Roman rule in Britain a suitable frontier in the North. The tidal waters were not easy to cross and the first Roman Bridge — Pons Aelii was at the place later called **NEWCASTLE.**

Here the new Norman Castle looked down on the river crossing from what had been the site of the Roman fort. The best view of the site is from the river or the bridge, giving a better impression of its height. The building of the railway viaduct and tall edifices, the filling of areas of the river bank lessen the impact obtained from old prints.

In medieval times the Castle dominated a walled town and was the symbol of medieval power. It was the key to Northumberland, and was for centuries associated with the county in government and military matters.

William I was here in 1072 while campaigning against Malcolm Canmore, King of Scots. In 1080 he sent his son Robert Curthose (short legs) against the Scots, and he was responsible for the first "new castle". Very likely a wooden bridge used the piers of the Roman bridge and so the Roman site was chosen to guard it. This was on a promontory precipitous on all sides except the west. The Lort burn and its tributary had cut deep ravines in their course to the river. Much of these have been filled, but there are still some breathtaking ascents and dizzy descents to and from the Castle compound.

Robert's Castle was defended by a palisade and ditch. The gateway on the west had multiple defences. There was also a mound or motte within the Castle, at the east end of the bailey. It has disappeared like the early stone walls that replaced the palisade. The Norman postern leading down to the Tyne is part of the early work. In Stephen's reign King David of Scotland was granted the earldom of Northumberland, which may have included the castles of Bamburgh and Newcastle.

Newcastle Castle was in a dilapidated condition when Henry II recovered it in 1157. It was greatly strengthened by the construction of stone walls and new gates. The great keep was planned and, in 1174, William the Lion of Scotland found it too strong to besiege without artillery. He came to Newcastle as a prisoner after his capture at Alnwick.

Work on the great keep, one of the finest in the country, began in 1172 and was completed in 1177 at a cost of £911" 10" 9d — a lot of money in those days. The architect was Master Maurice, who also built Dover Castle. Both keeps still stand four square. King John was not satisfied with his father's work and built a shell keep on the motte. The keep was now called the "old Tower". Henry III next built the new hall on the east side of the bailey, replacing the Norman Hall which was on the south side.

All these have disappeared, replaced by Council Offices and the Moot Hall. In 1247 the building of a fine barbican called the Black Gate was begun. It has been described as an "elaborately constructed and exceptional type." The ground floor was simple — a central passage with flanking towers containing guardrooms. The towers flank the whole of the gateway, and each has a vaulted chamber on the ground floor with loops commanding the ditch. The upper part of the gatehouse has been altered, but originally had flanking towers that may have been taken as a model for Dunstanburgh. The entrance was further protected by an outer barbican in 1358. It had gates, portcullis and drawbridge out front as well as a second line of defence. Defenders could produce flanking fire on attackers along a considerable length of curtain wall. The Black Gate is currently used as a Museum and can be visited in conjuction with the Keep, which is also open to the public.

The Keep is a massive structure measuring 62 feet by 56 feet and standing 75 feet high, which makes it a grandstand for viewing parts of Newcastle, the river Tyne and the network of railways. Steam power which blackened the masonry for so long has gone in favour of diesel oil and electricity. The Keep has a broad spreading plinth or base with tall buttresses seeming to add to its strength. At the top on each corner is a projecting turret — 3 square in shape and the N.W. one multangular, probably to take a catapult. The buttress on the west front is larger and provided the latrine shaft, away from the courtyard. The doors and windows are round arched with Norman ornamentation.

The entrance is on the east front, where stands a forework or extension. It had three towers, but the lower tower has disappeared. Steps lead to a door in the middle tower and further steps lead to a platform covered by the upper tower. The entrance to the Keep is on the second floor or third storey — further covering fire could be provided from the top of the Keep. This made the entrance very strongly defended. The constable's chamber was at the top of the stair, and he controlled entrance to the Royal rooms. The main room is the King's Hall, spacious and lofty. There was originally another storey above this and a pointed roof, as shown in the stonework, later replaced by a leaded platform roof. The King's Hall had a fine fireplace and a vaulted room for the well, from which water could be poured into pipes leading to a cistern and the cellars. The well was about 100 feet in depth. There were garderobes in the thickness of the wall; and in the south wall was the King's Chamber with a fine fireplace and windows looking out on the Tyne. In the N.W. turret with a barred door was a vaulted prison for superior people. At the S.E. corner a door opens into the main stair of the Keep, which leads to the spiral stair giving access to upper apartments and the parapet, and to lower apartments and the cellars. On the first floor below is the Queen's Hall with apartments corresponding to the King's above. The Queen's Chamber is in the north wall, not the south. Two wall chambers at different levels would weaken the structure of the Keep. The Queen's Hall had a fireplace, windows and a privy. The Queen's apartments could only be reached through the King's and this gave privacy. The upper storey was for the use of the soldiery who defended the Castle and were ready to take up positions on the battlements at a moment's notice. Down the winding stair the basement or cellars are reached. There is a fine Norman pillar in the centre from which springs 8 semi-circular ribs that support the vaulting. The cellar was dry and fire proof, providing protection for supplies. In the S.E. corner was the prison with a privy, and a vaulted storeroom between the Keep and the forework. On the west side a postern was opened for convenience of getting in stores — otherwise it would be up the stairs and down the stairs with a great deal of effort. The walls of the basement are enormously thick and the Keep's survival shows their strength. Through the central pillar water was piped to the basement.

In the upper part of the King's Hall a vaulted gallery runs through all four sides of the tower with loopholes and doors leading to the floor of the upper flat that no longer exists.

In the N.E. corner is a second spiral stair to the battlements and a straight stair in the wall to the entrance of the King's Hall. This would provide extra access and ease of movement for the men to and from the battlemets. It might confuse an enemy that got within the walls. By about 1250 the roof had been made flat and covered with lead. Lead was often laid on a bed of sand as a precaution against fire. The flat deck would provide a platform for catapults, used by defenders as well as attackers.

The last place to be mentioned, but in many ways the most interesting is the lovely Norman chapel. It had originally an outside entrance to serve the general household of the Castle and no internal access from the Keep till later. It has ribbed vaulting, wall arcading and a chancel arch of remarkable workmanship. There are strong similarities to the chapel of Durham Castle — the waterleaf ornamentation of the capitals. The chapel is T-shaped with the nave running N.S. at right angles to the chancel. The interior especially of the basement may seem gloomy, but other buildings now reduce the light, and in medieval times interiors would be plastered and whitewashed or painted. They also had their lights and any but narrow openings were dangerous.

TOWN WALLS OF NEWCASTLE

In medieval times Newcastle was a walled town — walls were constructed in the reign of Edward I and after. Murage or wall tax was paid by burgesses to maintain them. Newcastle was "fined" by Edward III for not maintaining its walls, though murage had been collected. The complete circuit of the town walls was more than two miles in length; and the shape of the enclosure has been likened to a knight's helmet with the neckpiece on the riverbank. The Castle with its own enclosure commanded the bridge. The town walls had 7 main gates and 19 towers with interval turrets, much in the manner of the Roman Wall. Within the walls were some 6 friaries, 6 hospitals and 6 churches, besides the chapel in the Tower. There were wealthy burgesses who had left their mark. Robert Rhodes was the improver of churches, and in particular the steeple of St. Nicholas was finished with its famous crown. Roger Thornton, the Dick Whittington of Newcastle, is remembered by the only surviving medieval brass in Northumberland. Once in All Saints, it is now in St. Nicholas Cathedral — a reminder of medieval wealth, life, death and religion.

The walls were battered by the Scots in the siege of 1644 and have been bulldozed by urban expansion; but parts remain that can be explored on foot.

Along the line of the Roman Wall, **Benwell** was the first Roman fort from Newcastle, and near it was the later Benwell Tower. It had belonged to Tynemouth Priory until the Dissolution of the Monasteries. Occupied by Robert Blakeney, the last Prior, it was described as — "A Tower and other buildings and a garden and a close."

In 1608 Robert Shafto held "the Stone Tower, being the manor house and other edifices thereto belonging with garden and garth and close" — in all 3 acres. In the Shafto Book is a little sketch showing the tower with house attached. In 1831 it was bought by Thomas Crawhall, who knocked it down and built a grander place. In 1881 Mr Pease gave this for the Bishop of Newcastle's house and built another at Pendower for himself.

Newburn on Tyne, further westwards, was much used as a crossing place and the scene of battles.

Newburn Tower was built in the fifteenth Century with a vaulted basement and later a hall was added to it. The buildings were taken over for industrial purposes.

Still further westwards and on the south side of the Tyne appears the imposing edifice of **PRUDHOE CASTLE**. It greatly impressed the artist Turner, who made of it a most romantic picture.

The castle stands on a hill which rises steeply from the Tyne Valley and Ovingham on the other side of the river. The site was linked to higher ground on the south by a neck of land, which was severed by a deep ditch. On the eastern side a burn has cut a deep ravine, making it an excellent place for fortification. In fact there were earthworks here before the first castle, which was a motte and bailey type.

It had been constructed by Robert of Umfraville II. The mound was at the west end of the hill and protected by a ditch or ditches. The south side was protected by a deep moat which linked with the ravine to the east. On the north the steepness of the slope was a sufficient defence. It was on the south side that Odinel of Umfraville built the first stone gatehouse. William the Lion, King of Scotland, had a particular grudge against Odinel, who did not support his claim to the earldom of Northumberland. In 1173 he attacked the Castle, but it was too strong to be taken and he went away.

In 1174 he returned and subjected the Castle to three days of furious attack, but the Castle had been strengthened by stone walls. Once again the attack failed and the Scots in anger burnt the corn in the fields, savaged the gardens and hacked the apple trees in the orchards. The angry Lion King of Scotland was captured in Alnwick Park. After the siege local inhabitants were called upon to perform the customary duty of castle building or repairing since much damage had been done. It was probably at this time that the great stone keep as at Newcastle was built, and in due course curtain walls were completed.

The Castle suffered severely in the Scottish Wars, but in 1381 it was acquired with other Umfraville property by the Earl of Northumberland, who married the widow of the Earl of Angus. After the 1405 rebellion Henry IV conferred Alnwick, Prudhoe and Langley on his son John, later Duke of Bedford. The Earl of Northumberland did not recover Prudhoe till 1441, and it changed hands in the Wars of the Roses. It was acquired by Henry VIII in 1537, but restored to the Earl of Northumberland in 1557 by Queen Mary and it was rented to Thomas Bates. A survey of 1596 describes Prudhoe as " an old Ruinous Castle, walled about, situate upon a high Moate of Earth, with ditches . . ."

It mentions two gates and without "a Turne Pyke".

The gatehouse was vaulted and had a chapel above it. Within the walls joining the north wall of the Castle was a Hall 18 yards long and 9 yards wide, suffering decay in lead and timber. To the left of the entrance was another house measuring 23 yards long and 6 yards wide. It contained a number of chambers and linked to the great Tower or keep. There was a passage to the chapel, and on the other side of the south wall to "a house called the Nursery". There was a garner, stables and a tower to the west.

The great tower measured 18 yards by 12 yards, and was three stories high. Among other buildings was a kitchen at the east end of the hall, and there was also a brewhouse. Outside the walls was an "Elder Chappell", now used for residence and cattle. There was also a mill at the castle gate. The orchard was spoilt, and later with the Earl in the Tower of London, the estate suffered from further neglect.

It was restored by the 2nd Duke of Northumberland for his son, who became Baron Percy of Prudhoe and lived there from 1816.

"The ruinous walls of the Hall, Kitchen, Nursery, Garner and Stable are taken away — The dwelling house has been rebuilt and enlarged."

The east end of the enclosure became a garden and the stables were rebuilt. A new garden was made outside the Castle to the south, taking in the area of the old chapel. This was what Turner saw, and some writers have considered that the Castle, 150 feet above the river, deserves the title "Proud height", although not etymologically accurate.

The Castle is approached from the south, where a medieval one arched bridge spans the burn. To the west was the mill pond and the two moats within which was the base court. These were converted into gardens, taking in the site of St. Mary's Chapel. The barbican in front of the gatehouse was added from 1326. It is 36 feet long, 24 feet wide, and had an inner passage through it 11 feet wide. The entrance is a covered gateway with a barrel vault. Then there was a drawbridge over the inner moat, worked from a covered building projecting 20 feet in front of the gatehouse. The gatehouse measures 18½ feet from north to south, and 30 feet from east to west. It has a round arched gateway with thick walls that contain no guard rooms. The passage, which rises steeply, is covered by vaulting. There was no portcullis. The chamber above the gatehouse was converted into a chapel, measuring 24 feet by 14½ feet within the walls. It was approached by steep stairs. The roof of the chapel was lowered to take another room above called the Wardrobe in later times. There were battlements and cross loops for defensive purposes. An oriel window was added as a chancel.

The Castle was divided into two wards, but this has been obscured by building changes. The keep stands in the inner ward, which was extended in the thirteenth century to bring all within the curtain wall. The keep measures 41 feet from north to south and 44 feet from east to west, but a forebuilding extends this to 56 feet. The tower is now 45 feet to the parapet, but was once higher since the ground level has been raised. The walls are 9 feet thick, much broken in parts and only the S.W. complete with angle turret. The walls have angle and pilaster buttresses for strength.

The basement had two chambers with connections made to the old hall. The straight stairs in the forebuilding have gone, but in the south corner is a spiral stair to the battlements and other floors. There were two above the ground floor with windows and fireplaces. After the curtain was extended with round towers at the N.W. and S.W. corners, other buildings were constructed including the hall, and at the east end of it, a kitchen. These have gone and the foundations buried, but the north curtain wall retains evidence of their presence. Much was obliterated by the buildings of the Georgian house north to south across the whole area. The structures that were covered included the southward extension of the hall, which included buttery, parlour, outer chamber and inner chamber and connections with the Keep. The S.W. tower has gone, but the N.W. tower still stands with battlements above and cross loops below. The round tower, a later development, can be compared with the square solidity of the Keep.

In the north eastern part of the curtain wall, there is a lot of massive masonry, probably retaining twelfth century work, and at the east end is a square tower. Here a few yards of the battlements of the wall survive, and between the tower and the gatehouse is a garderobe, one of several in the curtain walls.

Prudhoe Castle has been taken over by English Heritage, and after extensive renovations is now open to the public. Excavations have taken place at the east end and foundations revealed. It is an exciting place and there is much to be discovered.

North of Prudhoe and in hostile relationship to it was **Nafferton Castle,** situated off the A69, where it crosses the Whittle Burn. This Burn and its tributary carved ravines on the south and east sides of the site. On old O.S. maps it is marked Lonkin's Hall and associated with the monster of the ballad. It had an unsavoury reputation for other reasons. It was acquired by Philip of Ulcotes, one of King John's leading henchmen. He and Hugh of Balliol took over the castles of Alnwick, Durham, Mitford, Norham, Newcastle and Prudhoe. They were very much disliked, and in 1218 Richard of Umfraville of Prudhoe complained that he was building a castle at Nafferton without licence to the damage of Prudhoe. It seems Philip kept on building, but in 1221 the King directed the sheriff to dismantle the castle. Small timbers were to go to Newcastle to build a gaol, and the large timbers and "breteschia" to defend the gate at the bridge which had fallen.

Bates describes "breteschia" as embattled wooden erections of several stories which could be used for either attack or defence. The timber castle at Nafferton was demolished and the stonework there was of a later period. It was not mentioned in 1415. Excavations and investigation showed that a 27 feet square tower at the south end of the site was late medieval. There were other stone structures of later date than the rampart but it seems that Philip of Ulecotes had set up some stone walling. As at Welton, stone may have come from the Roman Wall; and much of the tower was still standing at the beginning of this century, but today very little.

WELTON TOWER AND HALL.

Welton is north of Nafferton and near the Whittledean Reservoirs. The stone of the tower is obviously taken from the Roman Wall, a short distance away. It is situated to the N.W. of the hall and surrounded by farm buildings. To the west is the medieval deserted village of Welton. The tower measures 24 feet by 20 feet, with walls 5 feet thick. The original entrance from the east is blocked. There was a stair to the floor above and there was yet another floor. Indications are that the tower had battlements and turret. There was building east of the tower, and it seems in the early seventeenth century extensive rebuilding was carried out. The hall extends from north to south — 55 feet by 25 feet with a big chimney on the west side and wing 35 feet by 20 feet on the south east. There is a door head inscribed W W 1614 — the name of William Welton. It shows how a medieval hall attached to a tower was converted into a more convenient residence.

The profile is very different from **Halton Tower,** near the Roman Wall at Halton Chesters and built from Roman stone. Here too is a village that has almost disappeared. The early buildings of Halton were burned by the Scots in 1297. In 1382, however, there is mentioned a fortlet of Halton, belonging to Robert de Lowther. It was later acquired by William de Carnaby, and in 1415 he was the owner of the tower.

It had other buildings attached to it and there was also a barmkin. The tower measures roughly 31 feet by 24½ feet with walls 5 feet thick. The basement was vaulted, lit by one loop. The entrance was from the N.W. corner with two doors and a wall stair leading to the first floor, which has a fireplace on the west side with windows on the south and east. These have been enlarged and there are small wall chambers in the S.W. and S.E. angles. The spiral stair was in the N.E. angle, and the garderobe in the N.W. This applied to the other floors, which retain the original windows. At roof level each corner carries a corbelled bartizan and each of these has a small room, except the one with the stair.

In the fifteenth century a manor house was erected on the north side of the tower, and the complex of buildings assumed a T shape with the tower at the base. The apartments can be determined from an inventory taken at the death of Lancelot

Carnaby in 1624. It gives the rooms and their contents. In the tower the rooms are described as the low tower, the middle tower and the high tower. These are all above the basement and from the contents were all used as bedrooms. The main entrance was at the top of the T, and the door from the north led to passage forming the screens. On the left was the buttery and kitchen, which has disappeared; on the right was a Hall with a Parlour and Mr Carnaby's Chamber, which had a loft above. Between these apartments and the tower was the Great Chamber. This contained a long table, 18 buffet stools, a pair of virginalls, several "cubberts", cubbert cloths, "halfe a score of cushions and 3 long cushins for the windows". This shows that the Great Chamber had window seats and gives the impression of considerable comfort. There was "One Blacke chayer" worth 3s 4d The other rooms were the high chamber and the adjoining chamber, both bedrooms. Some of the beds were obviously four posters "with courtings and vallance". In the butler's chamber and kitchen chamber there were more beds — 2 for the butler and 7 in the kitchen chamber. The original windows still remain in what were the butler's chambers, but the kitchen has gone.

The range of farm buildings further north probably include what were brewhouse, bakery and stores. The Carnabys were a family of considerable importance. Sir William Carnaby of Halton Tower was MP for Morpeth in 1623 and 1640. In 1642 he was expelled from Parliament as a Royalist and fought for the King at Marston Moor. His lands were confiscated and he never seems to have regained full prosperity. He was buried in the chapel adjacent to the Hall.

In the later part of the seventeenth century an extension was made to the east of the tower in the spirit and style of Capheaton or Bockenfield, which suggests Robert Trollope, but no definite date has been given for this. The forecourt has a pillared gateway and the chimneys have been built as high as the tower to obtain the necessary draught. In 1695 Halton was bought by John Douglas, whose daughter and heiress married Sir Edward Blackett. Blacketts still live at Halton.

Visible from Halton is **Aydon Castle,** which was sold 1653/4 by the Carnabys to William Collison.

Aydon, now in the care of English Heritage, is the next place to visit. The property was acquired by Robert de Raymes in 1296, who came from Suffolk seeking his fortune. He fought against the Scots under Sir Henry Percy. In 1305 he obtained licence from Edward I to crenellate his manor houses at both Aydon and Shortflat in view of the danger from the Scots. In 1315 the Scots took the Castle and burnt it. In 1317 it was again ravaged and Robert claimed losses of £1000. His annual income of £50 was reduced to nothing. He was granted some compensation and was appointed collector of customs at Newcastle and Hartlepool. He was also an MP.

Later the Raymes ceased to live at Aydon and it went into disrepair.
It was leased to the Shaftos and from 1541 Cuthbert Carnaby lived there. He made repairs and from 1653 William Collison made changes. The west range was converted into stables. Both families have left their marks at Aydon.

The site had natural advantages for defence — shaped like a pentagon, the Aydon Burn flows round three sides from the north to the south west. The burn has carved a ravine and the slopes are precipitous. The south side looks into an abyss and the first buildings were here. The enclosed area is about an acre, divided into an outer bailey and inner court.

Aydon Castle or Hall was essentially a manor house, which from the necessities of the time and place had to be fortified. The early hall house may well have been timbered; the main plan being solar, hall and kitchen quarters. By 1296 the building was in stone and cruciform in shape. It consisted of two stories with the hall on the first floor, approached by outside steps. There would be a protective wall to the north. A penthouse roof covered the steps and a door, secured by a stout bar, opened to the screens. The hall was to the left and the kitchen to the right. (You can still make this approach).

The Hall measured 31 feet long, 25 feet wide and 16 feet high. The dais was at the east end, lit by windows of two lights, and the windows had stone seats. Above the screens was the minstrels' gallery. The kitchen retains two original windows, but much has been altered and the fireplace bears the Carnaby arms.

A doorway at the east end of the hall leads to the solar, or private quarters. This measures 47½ feet long by 18 feet wide. It has 4 original double light windows, all with seats. The hooded fireplace has been moved from the east side where it was to the opposite side. Partition walls have been removed — there would be apartments for the lord and his wife and perhaps a chapel. This disposes of the idea that there was a chapel in the eastern extension of the building, since this contained garderobes, sinks and drains. On the ground floor below the hall were store rooms, and the main apartment has a

Bywell Castle

Welton Tower and Hall

Bedlington Old Hall

Vicar's Pele, Corbridge

West Bitchfield Tower

Belsay Castle when inhabited

Aydon Castle – Medieval Chimney

fireplace, which was served by a magnificent original chimney outside; it is circular with a conical top in which are pointed smoke-holes. There are other rooms underneath the solar and one apartment had an ornamented fireplace.

After 1305 Reymes, with permission to crenellate and fortify, made additions to the buildings. A west range was built out from the old kitchen and store. This had a vaulted basement, and the kitchen was transferred to the first floor of this wing. It contained a great fireplace and wall cupboards. At a higher level and perhaps above a floor that has gone can be seen a series of holes for pigeons. In the north east angle is a kind of guard room with slits looking outside the inner bailey and into it. A door gives access to a rampart walk along the north and east walls that enclose the inner bailey. These walls are 4½ feet thick and are battlemented. Embattled parapets were also added to the main buildings. Water is carried from the roof by a line of gargoyle spouts on both north and south sides.

The final stages of fortification were the construction of the curtain walls to enclose the outer bailey. These are 5 feet thick and vary in height from 10 to 25 feet according to the nature of the ground. The pentagonal shape is deliberately designed.

The S.W. corner provided a square courtyard with the north wall joining the west wing. Then there is an area projecting 16 feet, which was made up of buildings on either side of the entrance. The postern was in the S.W. angle and the wall was protected by a moat. There was presumably a drawbridge. At the N.W. angle of the projection was a square tower with garderobes. The northern apex of the enclosure had another tower — rounded outwards and square inside. The two eastern walls are not so high, because they cover the precipitous fall into the Aydon Burn. Only on the N.W. side would it have been possible for the enemy to use siege engines. The eastern curtain walls have holes which could have taken a timber fighting gallery.

In the Carnaby period when restoration took place the sixteenth century fireplace in the old kitchen was given their arms (two bars, in chief 3 roundlets). The Collisons W.C. & H.C. 1653 appear on the lintel of the present ground floor entry to the house, and W.C. 1657 over the door of the west range which became stables and cowbyre. Before being taken over by English Heritage, Aydon Castle was a working farmhouse and it would be interesting for the various parts to be recorded.

CORBRIDGE

Aydon shows how a peaceful country house was fortified to meet the perils of the Scottish Wars; and to the south in Corbridge churchyard by the church, we see how the parson coped with the same problem. The building, of Roman stone, is the best example of this type to inspect. It was never embodied in another house and has not been altered. Today it is the centre for Tourist Information in Corbridge.

The tower is not large — it measures 27 feet by 21 feet rising to a height of 30 feet. The parapet adds 5 further feet of masonry. This is embattled and carried round the corners on projecting corbels. The basement is a vaulted cellar entered by a door on the east side and lit by a slit at the west end. The walls are 4½ feet thick. A wall stair from the door rises to the first floor which was the priest's parlour or living room, with a good fireplace and windows with seats. There was a garderobe in the N.E. corner and lockers or wall cupboards. At the top of the stairs is a stone table and sink set in the wall. A stair continues from the garderobe corner to the second floor, which was timbered with beams supported on corbels. This was the study and bedroom. There were three windows; one on each side of the N.E. corner, where there was a stone book rest. While at his "desk", the vicar could look out to the Roman fort, and through his north window to a church tower, built of Roman stone. We do not know whether the vicar ever took to the battlements to defend his tower. It had embrasures, closed by swinging shutters between the merlons. Below, the only entry to the tower, was a strong wooden door with bar and protected on the outside by an iron grate as at **Bywell.**

Corbridge had other towers, one is Low Hall at the east end of Main Street. It measures 24 feet by 18 feet with a vaulted basement and two stories above. The entrance was on the west side with the spiral stair in the N.W. corner. At a later stage a hall was added to the west of the tower and the fenestration was altered. A small square tower was added to the north of the tower. It is called Baxter's tower, since it was built probably by Baxter probably in the fifteenth century. There are other old houses which could be described as the bastle type.

The next castle on the Tyne to view is **Bywell,** an interesting place not far from the river crossing, with two churches both of Saxon origin. It now has a castle, hall, rectory and a few houses, but in former times it could be described as a town. In 1570 a survey ran —

"The towne of Bywell ys buylded in lengthe all in one strete upon the ryver or water of Tyne" . . . divided into two parishes and inhabited by "handy craftesmen whose trade is all in yron work for the horsemen and borderers of that country as the making of byttes, styroppes, buckles and such others, wherein they are expert and conying and are subject to the incursions of the theaves of Tynedale and compelled winter and somer to brying all their cattell and sheepe inyo the strete in the night season and watch both endes of the strete and when the enemy approchity to raise the hue and cry whereupon all the toune prepareth for rescue of their goodes which is very populous by reason of their trade and stoute and hardy by contynuall practyse ageynst the'enemy."

In that same year 1570 there were 15 shops in Bywell held at the will of the lord. The report says that in Bywell the ancestors of the Earl of Westmorland, who had forfeited his estates for rebellion, "buylded a faire tourw or gatehouse all of stone and covered with leade, meaning to have proceded further as the foundations declare being the height of a man above ground which were never fynyshed and the said toure is a good defence for the towne and will sonn decaye if it be not mayntened".

In 1608 it was still royal property, but plundered by "wasters and spoylers", and the trees were being felled by the 100. The castle had been robbed of its lead and the timbers were rotten. The fisheries here were also being frequently poached, and the dam was broken. The property came into the hands of the Fenwicks about 1630, and was sold in 1820 to the Beaumont family, who still own hall, castle and estate.

The Castle was built in the fifteenth century by Ralph Nevill, who became Earl of Westmorland. It was at the east end of the village, and its purpose seems to have been, with its unfinished barmkin, to provide local inhabitants with protection against robbers and raiders. They made ironware, leather ware and other equipment that attracted thieves. King Henry VI took refuge in the Castle for a time in 1464. The entire emphasis of the Castle was upon the gatehouse, which was very strongly built. It measures about 60 feet by 40 feet and stands very close to the north bank of the river. It was protected by a portcullis and had double doors of oak. The entrance is about 11 feet wide, and at the north end of the tunnel vault are doors into chambers or guardrooms on either side. On the west side is a door leading to the stair, which was protected by a "yett" or door reinforced by a complicated iron grille, in which the bars interlap. At the top of the stair is a meutriere or murder hole to threaten the enemy.

The chamber on the first floor measures 30 feet by 23 feet with another 20 feet by 23 feet. The dividing wall may not be original. Both parts have fireplaces in the north wall. The garderobe is in the S.W. corner, and the portcullis groove in the middle of the south front. The stair continues to the upper chamber 50 feet long, which has two fireplaces, two windows on each of the long sides and one to east and west.

The stair ends with an umbrella vault and leads to the battlements with machicolation over the entry. Each corner has a turret,

"cleverly converted into octagons by having their battlements supported on long stones overhanging the angles".

A long piece of curtain wall to the east of the gatehouse still survives. The old market cross between the castle and the churches is all that remains of the old town which had 15 shops.

Bywell Hall was built in the mid eighteenth century to the designs of Paine. Wallis describes the area of what was the village — "in a bounded, low, but delightful situation, beautifully rural, by the banks of the river Tyne, having a grass lawn before it to the south . . . adorned with stately oaks and other forest trees."

In a similar area, south of the Tyne and overlooking the Devilswater, is **Dilston Tower,** and the village to the east of it has gone. It epitomises two centuries of Northumberland's history. In 1415 the castle does not appear on the list, so the manor house was then unfortified. Its position probably provided some protection, and the tower may have been built from 1417 when Sir William Claxton took over.

It measured about 40 feet by 23 feet with a vaulted basement. The entrance was at the NE corner and the spiral staircase in the N.W. There were two floors above, but the building has been very much altered. An addition measuring 14 feet by 13 feet was made at the south end, entered from the other tower. This like the basement had loops for air, light and defence. It contained 3 floors above the basement. Later, in the sixteenth century, an addition was made on the north side, covering the old entrance and containing a range of four floors. Still further north was another range of buildings that contained the 'old hall', the great chamber and other apartment. New windows and fireplaces were added making it into an Elizabethan house. There were further alterations and additions in the seventeenth century, but this was not enough for the Earl of Derwentwater, who had much of it demolished and built another mansion, which was never finished and demolished after the Rebellion of 1715. Only the chapel, where he was buried, and the gaunt remains of the old tower and hall still stand a memorial to the Earl of Derwentwater — executed in 1716.

The S.W. area of the county were sparsely populated, except in the great days of leadmining. Almost on the Durham border is **Blanchland,** which always appears as a planned village by Lord Crewe. The plan was determined by the layout of the monastery which existed in medieval times, and was a great asset to travellers in these parts. The snow lies longer here, but this does not give rise to the name.

"Blanchland" came from the Praemonstratensian Abbey in France that founded the convent here — the same order as at Hulne Priory, Alnwick. In 1327 Blanchland was sacked by the Scots, and when King Edward III was there they asked him for food and compensation. In 1539 the monastery was dissolved and the monks were pensioned. The lands were purchased by William Farewell, whose widow married Anthony Radcliffe and whose daughter married Cuthbert, Anthony's son. The property later passed to the Forster family and then to Lord Crewe, Bishop of Durham in 1704. He also obtained Bamburgh Castle and restored both properties.

Part of the Church remains and is used for religious purposes. Other monastic buildings are embodied in the "Lord Crewe Arms", providing the hospitality that the monastery once did. The north end of the hotel was the abbot's tower. It measures about 40 feet by 20 feet, and is strongly built. Next to it was the guesthouse and the kitchen, and there is evidence of vaulted basements. To the west of the tower was the gatehouse, which still stands, but has suffered from rebuilding. It measures 45 feet by 20 feet, and the arched tunnel of the gateway is about 10 feet wide. Walls linked it to the tower and other monastic buildings to complete the enclosure.

Within the Church are interesting grave covers — one of an abbot and another of James Eggleston, who was a forester. Inscribed on his slab are a sword, an arrow and a hunting horn. Houses of the village have been built about the cloister square, which is an extended market place. It has been described as one of the best examples of a planned village in England.

Hexhamshire belonged to the Archbishop of York, and in 1542 there is a report,
"About the beginning of April they take the most part of there cattell and go with them up into the highlands and there buildeth them lodges and sheeles, until the month of August."
This meant that there were few permanent habitations and a dearth of towers, since they depended on the remoteness and difficulty of the country. One of the few remnants of medieval masonry can be found at Dotland Park, where there was a hunting lodge of the Archbishop of York. The Bishop of Durham had a large game reserve in Stanhope Park, at times plundered by the Scots.

Hexham itself is a suitable place at which to finish a survey of fortified places. Here were the headquarters of the Archbishop of York for Hexhamshire, adjacent to the Abbey on top of a hill and overlooking the Tyne valley. The original Church went back to the time of Bishop Wilfrid and was built from Roman stone. The crypt was the refuge for sacred relics, and later the Abbey itself a sanctuary, but never safe from the Scots.

The danger was not only from the Scots, because men of the shire had a reputation for lawlessness. It was alleged that the franchise of the Archbishop enabled criminals to escape the law of the land. Hexham had two towers belonging to the Archbishop. In 1330 there was an order for a suitable gaol to be built to detain offenders. It was provided with chains, manacles and all other things necessary. The gaoler was John, the barber, who was paid 2d a day.

The tower called the Moot Hall was probably built later. In 1355 the manorial offices were said to be very dilapidated, and it may well be that the Moot Hall was built. In 1415 one tower is mentioned, probably because both were within the same walled enclosure and regarded as a castle. The Moot Hall is very much a gate house type of structure, controlling access to the Archbishop's enclosure.

In Lord Dacre's time the gaol was kept full, but in 1538 a gang of outlaws broke in and rescued their fellows. The gaol was damaged and in 1550 both towers were reported as being in decay. The gaol was used to keep prisoners as late as 1824, and the Moot Hall used as a court house until 1838. The two buildings with a wall on top of the steep hill were in the nature of a castle, and a curtain wall went round them. The Moot Hall was the gateway to the bailey, and was provided with three pairs of gates and there were towers at the angles of the bailey. The hill top area was defended before the construction of the gaol. It is interesting to notice that this was built entirely out of Roman stone from Corstopitum, whereas the Moot Hall had to be constructed from fresh quarried stone; the Roman supply was exhausted.

The Moot Hall is a T shaped building — the length being north to south and the top being east to west — the west facing out to the town. The wings on either end of the top of the T provided small rooms for the soldier guards and their stores. This part rises higher than the length of the T, which had battlements supported by three stage corbels. The corbels still remain, but walls have been built above them to take a flat leaded roof. The vaulted entrance passage was constructed like a barbican with two western gates, one within the other and a third gate on the bailey side. At each side above the gate is a relieving arch supporting an outer wall and providing a space that could be used in the same way as machicolation for dropping liquids and solids on the heads of attackers. Above these were the small rooms, reached by the newel stair in the east angle of the bailey gate. This is shown by six windows one above the other to a turret that is the highest part of the building. On the north of the entrance was the vaulted basement measuring 20 feet by 30 feet which was used for stores. Above this and the tunnel entrance were the main apartments — the hall measured 46 feet by 20 feet wide. This was used for purposes of justice and a chamber of similar size above provided accommodation for the bailiff. Other buildings such as the kitchen, buttery and brewhouse within the bailey have disappeared as well as the curtain walls. Altogether the Moot Hall is a very impressive building, now used for municipal purposes and the basement for exhibitions.

The gaol by contrast is a much more regular shape of building — rectangular. It still retains remarkably its full quota of 63 corbels — 20 on each long side and 12 on each of the shorter sides. The battlements that they once carried have disappeared, somewhat spoiling the proportions. Nevertheless it is an impressive building, now used as the Middle March Museum and a Tourist Information Centre. The entrance is on the west side and the small lights indicate the ascent of the newel stair. The ground floor is vaulted, and there is a descent into what was the prison beneath. The original windows remain in the upper storey. At ground level a plinth surrounds the building and at a higher level moulding makes its way around the structure. It might seem strange that the old school was near the prison house, but it has now changed — its function is to attract visitors and not to detain unwilling boarders.

The Middle March Centre attempts to illustrate the troubled life of the Border at the time of the Reivers and when Lord Dacre filled the prison with offenders. Illustrations of their weaponry, armour, habitations and customs are shown as well as the arms of local families.

Conclusions

The building of castles and towers in Northumberland covers a period of some 500 years. Some of the original Norman castles continue to the present day.

The castles proper belonged to the King and the great barons, including the Archbishop of York and the Bishop of Durham. The lesser barons had smaller residences or mansions. The most usual was the hall house with a series of apartments at ground level and above.

With the increased danger from Scotland tower houses were built in which apartments were constructed one above the other. The owners obtained licence to crenellate, and walled enclosures were constructed called barmkins. The term 'pele' is a later term applied to the enclosure and not the tower.

Clergymen were not immune from attack and built their defensive towers. Monasteries were liable to plunder and had gatehouses with walled enclosures.

A number of castles were of the courtyard type with a large tower at each corner, linked by curtain walls. No two castles are the same, and differences range from the great drum towers at Dunstanburgh to the sophisticated structure on top of the motte at Warkworth.

Tower houses with vaulted basements for stores and livestock were for lesser men, and still later, from about 1550 dozens of strong houses called 'bastles' were built. This was because local men had to defend their families against raiders from the Border, Redesdale or Tynedale. It was not a matter for armies and the authorities found it very difficult to raise men, "furnished" with arms for the musters.

Fortifications were expensive to maintain, and many were neglected from the Crown properties downwards. The aristocracy of Northumberland were mostly absentees, and the upper gentry had to provide leadership and local service. "All in all few buildings of outstanding architectural merit were constructed in Northumberland during the first quarter of the seventeenth century. This fact reminds us of the remoteness of the county and the relative poverty of its leading families." Watt.

It could be added that their chief residences were outside the county.

Addenda

The basement of a bastle or tower was not just a stable or cowshed. It would be a place for storage of food for people and animals and also fuel. Corn would be stored for food and seed. Cattle would be kept, but others would be killed and salted for preservation. Salt was a most valuable product from the local salt pans, made by evaporating brine from the sea. The Bishop of Durham and the monasteries of Newminster and Tynemouth had their salt pans. Fish and eels were consumed in large quantities, especially by the religious. Some game was available, but deer were the preserve of the King and nobility. Large areas of "Forest" were under special law. They were woodland areas but nothing like the serried ranks of conifers set by the Forestry Commission in modern times. Woods were protected, but fallen timber could be gathered. Fuel could be provided by cutting turf or peat. Dried animal dung was also used and in some places coal.

Sheep were milked, but by far the most important product in those days was "the golden fleece", hence the Lord Chancellor's seat was a "woolsack". The monastic granges had huge flocks of sheep.

Chibburn Preceptory is near Druridge Bay and for years a ruin in an opencast coal site. It is a strange reminder of the passage of time. The building in medieval times belonged to the Knights of St. John of Jerusalem, consisting of a moated residence with a chapel. After 1540 it became the property of the Widdringtons and was converted into a manor house. Hodgson wrote—
"The old mansion house of Low Chibburn has been defended by a moat and barmkin. It is a massive old fashioned building with a chimney like a huge buttress projecting from its south gable."
The mansion house had two storeys and the windows of the second storey projected on corbels. The chapel was built of excellent ashlar and had another floor added. Over the entrance were eroded escutcheons with crosses and a floriated cross decorated a medieval grave slab which was used as a threshold stone.

It is hoped that this building can be saved and perhaps used as a visitors' centre for the threatened Druridge Bay.

Books and References

Archaelogis Aeliana	1944 Early Castles, 1949 Dunstanburgh, 1950 Castles from the Air, 1951 Haughton, 1954 Warkworth, 1955 Mitford, 1958 Alnwick.
Barley and St. Joseph	Medieval England from the Air
Bates, Cadwallader J.	Border Holds of Northumberland, 1891.
Brown, R. A.	Architecture of Castles. English Medieval Castles.
English Heritage Guides	Aydon, Berwick, Belsay, Dunstanburgh, Norham, Prudhoe, Tynemouth, Warkworth.
Plantagenet Sonerset Fry	Castles 1980

Gascoigne, B.	Castles of Britain
Graham, F.	Castles of Northumberland
H. M. S. O.	Shielings and Bastles
Hodgson, J.	History of Northumberland
Hugill, R.	Castles and Peles of the English Border
Forde Johnson, J.	Castles and Fortifications of Britain and Ireland.
Long, B.	Castles of Northumberland
Platt, C.	The Castle in Medieval England and Wales 1982
Pevsner, N.	Buildings of Northumberland
Rowland, T. H.	Medieval Castles of Northumberland 1969
Simpson, G. D.	Castles of England and Wales 1969
Hamilton Thompson, A.	Military Architecture in England during the Middle Ages 1912
Watts, S. J.	From Border Middle Shire, Northumberland 1982
Graham Fairclough	Information on Edlingham Castle

INDEX LIST

(M) Motte, (C) Castle 1415, (T) Fortalice 1415, (R) Ruinous, (D) Destroyed, (Occ) Occupied, (Op) Open to Public, (FP) Farm purposes, (EH) English Heritage, (NT) National Trust.

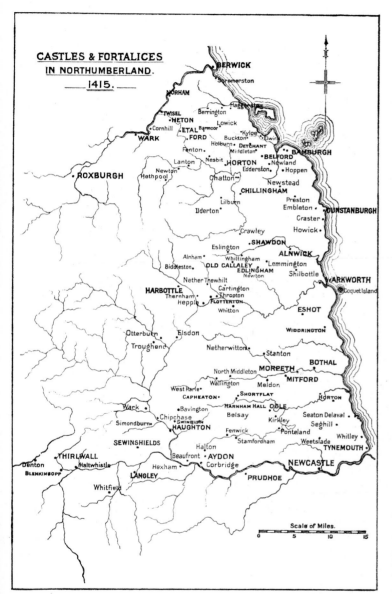

CASTLES & FORTALICES
IN NORTHUMBERLAND.
1415.

CASTLES TOWERS
BARMKINS & FORTRESSES
along the East & Middle Marches.
1541.